Schooner

Dorothy "Toots" LaFond

Part II of the

"Grandma Was A Sailor" Trilogy

By Captain Dorothy ("Toots") LaFond, ret.

Table of Contents

Preface

At the age of 56, my Aunt Toots (known to the rest of the world as Dorothy LaFond) took a job working as a crew member on the tall ship *Harvey Gamage.* Sailing up and down the east coast of North America during the summer and in the Caribbean during the winter, the ship paid its way by offering short voyages to groups interested in ocean sailing, whale watching, and related topics. In her first season on the ship, Toots worked her way up from crew to officer (purser), and became an instructor for celestial navigation. She also kept terrific journals recording her sailing experiences, which have been edited into this trilogy of books. Part I, "Snowbirds," covers the several months she worked as crew on the *Ann Marie*, sailing from Wisconsin to the Virgin Islands. This book, Part II, covers Toot's time on the schooner *Harvey Gamage,* offering a unique account of living and working on a modern tall ship, and of all the fascinating variety of weather, wildlife, and human life she encountered. Part III, "The *Norfolk Rebel*," will be issued as soon as we can find and edit that set of Toot's journals. Toots isn't sure where they are!

- *Ann Larkin Hansen, March 2017*

Introduction: How it all began

<u>April, 1991</u>

After getting married during college, I had six sons and two daughters in thirteen years. Though I'd always loved sailing I was occupied full time with the care and feeding of this menagerie until they grew up, and so didn't have much opportunity for sailing or travel. We did have a small boat in the lake across the road from our small farm that I sailed with and taught the kids in. But it wasn't until last year (1990), after I was invited along to help deliver a sailboat to the West Indies, that I finally got to walk on an ocean beach and experience salt water.

During that trip we came into Annapolis, Maryland on a cold evening in October, and I was excited to see a schooner parked at the end of the city dock.

After securing our boat we had dinner and then I talked my shipmate Kim into walking over to see her. We were leaving early the next morning for Beaufort, North Carolina, so it would be the only chance I'd have. Even though it was a miserable evening with a cold, wet, drizzle penetrating everything, we donned our foul weather gear and walked around the little harbor separating us from where she was tied.

The walk was worth it. She was incredible, even better than I had anticipated. We stood in the drifting mist and gazed up at those tall raked masts and the spider web rigging, glistening black with wet, gleaming in the light from the street lamps. The masts, the wide wood decks and the towering rigging were all saturated with rain, giving them a rich patina that made her look like a three dimensional painting.

We didn't dare step aboard but there was a light in one porthole so we hailed the ship. The mate came up to talk to us and explained that he was the only one aboard. He wasn't dressed for the weather and apologized for not giving us a tour or inviting us aboard. We talked for a brief time, I gave him my card, and as he started below to get out of the rain he invited us over in the morning to look around. There was nothing else to do but go back to our boat and warm up. I was glad we'd had a chance to get close enough for a good look

I forgot the incident until the following spring when I got a call from Eben, the owner of the boat, saying the mate from the *Harvey Gamage* had passed my card on to him and what did I have in mind?

To make a long story short I now have a job as crew on a 100-ton schooner and will be working on her as we sail up and down the east coast. I'm supposed to report aboard on May 13th in Gloucester, Massachusetts. I can't really believe it! Something will happen and the owner, who hired me over the phone, will take one look at this grey hair and decide that I'm not tough enough to handle a job working on a ship this size.

Doubts and second thoughts about the wisdom of what I'm doing keep floating up in my mind, but my daughters Barbie and Theresa seem to think it's a fantastic idea and have encouraged me to take this job. Barbie says it gives her hope that she will be able to do something similar after her boys are grown. Theresa's comment was that "there is life after kids."

Dry Dock

May 13, 1991: The Adventure Begins

It took me an hour and a half to drive to Gloucester from Rob's *(Toot's oldest son, then in the Coast Guard and stationed in Boston)* house and then I drove all around town trying to spot the *Harvey Gamage*. You'd think that finding a boat with tall masts would be easy, but Gloucester is a fishing port, and there are hundreds of boats docked around the harbor. The rigs on some of the trawlers are almost as tall as the masts on a sailing ship.

I finally located her tied to the pier between the schooners *Adventure* and *Pilot,* both looking like they were right out of "Captains Courageous" with the black hulls and classic lines of Grand Banks fishing schooners. Both of them were in the docks for extensive repairs. A lot of the planks on the hulls and decks needed replacement; the workers hoped both would be in the water and sailing by summer.

The *Harvey Gamage* didn't look much better than the other two when I stepped aboard. She was in for her annual dry dock period and everything below decks had been brought on deck to be inspected, sorted, and re-stored. It looks like a gypsy flea market. The empty interior is being cleaned and painted. Meanwhile there is extensive cleaning, sanding, oiling, chipping, rust busting, painting, and varnishing going on.

I was shown to a tiny little cabin where I dumped my gear and realized that I would have to repack again. I brought way too much stuff and there's not room to store anything.

I went on deck and was immediately assigned to Art Kimerely. He was working on the rigging and without delay put me to work taking the worming and parceling *(please see the glossary at the end of the book for definitions of nautical terms – ed.)* off the lower part of the main shrouds. Art used to own the Brigantine *Romance*, which he sailed twice around the world with his bride. I found out that he is a master rigger and I couldn't ask for a better teacher.

After we had cleaned all the tools and put the equipment from the day's work away under a big tarp on the deck, we used the same turpentine we used to clean the tools to scrub our hands to get the tar and dirt off. Mary Ellen, a woman about my age, had invited me to her cabin for a martini so I went to my cabin to change clothes and then went to hers. She is very happy to have another woman on board to share with. She has been running a tight ship (as purser, the officer in charge of bookkeeping and supplies) and knows where everything is and should be, but she has been on the *Harvey* for a year now and is ready to take a break. Right after the yard period she will leave for a family reunion in California.

Everyone is very friendly. Dave, the cook, is into astrology and wants to know everyone's birth sign. He wants to get together with the different crew members over "tea" and "do" their horoscopes. He should prove to be interesting to talk to. He's from Maine; a gourmet cook and a fabulous baker.

May 14

At six this morning when I got up, the deck of the boat was at least 12 feet below the dock. If I need to go ashore I will have to climb up on the rail and grab the shrouds so I can lean over and drop to the dock. Yesterday afternoon the boat was way above the dock and I had to step onto a piling and then down to the dock.

Right now I'm sitting on the "lister," a compartment amidships that covers the diesel engine used to power the generator and water pump. It has other compartments for storage built around the base and is a very pleasant place to sit. The weather is overcast but comfortable with gulls squawking and flying all around - they have a real feed when the fishing boats unload next to us and stuff gets spilled in the bay. The gulls are as big as chickens, soaring around and diving into the waste from the fish boats, or sitting on the dock and pilings complaining loudly that they were cheated out of some special morsel. They even land on the nets that are rolled up on big reels on the rigs and pick little fish and other weird looking sea life out of the mess.

The town is starting to wake up and the traffic noises are getting louder. The dock to the north of us is doing a booming business with huge baskets of fish being taken from the fishing boats and loaded onto a conveyor belt that goes into the warehouse. Meanwhile there is a stream of noisy ice shooting into their holds for the next trip out.

Lots of fishing boats are going in and out. They are either unloading baskets of fish or picking up ice and fuel. There is constant activity, lots of yelling back and forth and good natured banter. There is also a very distinctive odor of fish, fuel, and tidal flats that I think will always remind me of Gloucester.

A baby pigeon fell into the water. It was flapping its wings and thrashing about trying to fly, but couldn't get its wings out of the water. Then the sea gulls started diving on it. It didn't take long before a flock of screeching gulls pecked it to death and tore it into tiny little pieces, then each flew off with their portion to the nearest piling to ingest it. I couldn't scare them away and there was nothing I could do except feel bad. What a vicious racket! Finally all that was left were a few feathers floating on the now still water: nature can be brutal.

There are four tall ships in port, all in different stages of repair. The *Adventure* is having her decks reconstructed, and her whole stern is torn apart. The *Pilot* is up on the dry dock having planks replaced above the water line. This is one of the larger shipyards along the coast, with the equipment to drydock not only these huge schooners but also the big ocean going tugs that come in.

For now I have my cabin to myself. It's not very big but it has two bunk beds and a sink that folds down from the bulkhead. The only source of water for washing is a spigot that I have to pump by hand. There is a small shelf, a mirror, and some hooks on the wall. It does have a door for privacy, and I had a good sleep last night. There is a hole drilled through the deck above my bunk and it has a solid block of glass sealed into it so the light comes in but the water is still sealed out. It's amazing how much light that little piece of glass (8 inches across) lets into the cabin - it would be awful dark down here otherwise. The bunk room is about eight by eight feet and not an inch wasted. Everything is kept very primitive to keep the authentic atmosphere of a working coastal schooner.

Eben, the owner of the *Harvey Gamage*, will be aboard today to go over what needs to be done and it looks like a lot! The lines and rigging all have different names and I'm going to do some checking on my own to see which lines control which sail.

I really like this boat. She was built to the specs of an early coastal trader but is only 17 years old so she has the aura of an old boat but is very sound. We will be in Gloucester for three weeks doing maintenance on the boat and I will be trying to absorb all the new things going around me for a long time after that. This is a whole new way of life and I like it.

2200

Art and I have been chipping rust and old paint from the shrouds and turnbuckles for two days now. We have to loosen all the paint and rust with a chipping hammer in order to remove the turnbuckles. Then we brush them clean, and paint them with a rust-proofing silver paint that sticks to skin and clothes like glue.

The wrapping on the shrouds, from the top of the turnbuckles up to where the marlin is sound, comes off in a solid string and is removed in any way possible. Then we wire brush the steel cable and wipe it down with acetone. Then the cable has to be painted with the same rust proof paint, and after that dries it is coated with pine tar and wrapped with two-inch wide canvas, re-tarred, and wrapped again. Then the whole thing is served, or tightly wrapped with a type of twine starting at the top and wrapping down. Then it has to be painted with tar again! We have 24 of these to do! The saying goes, "worm and parcel with the lay, turn and serve the other way." I've heard this saying often but never really knew what it meant; it takes first-hand experience to really know. My hands look like I've been doing something extremely impressive: They're stained with rust, oil, silver paint, pine tar, and covered with a multitude of nicks and scratches. The fingernails that are left are imbedded with black gunk.

The *Theresa Marie*, a big trawler, parked next to us this evening and brought us a bag with four huge lobsters from a fresh catch. They will be next to us for a few days as they go out for 10 days at a time, and then are in for three. A Coast Guard patrol boat came in also - the station is just south of us a couple of piers down.

I can't believe how dirty my jeans are. I only brought two pair with me from Rob's, so after I changed into clean ones I saved the dirty ones for working in tomorrow. I tried to make some calls home tonight but no one was answering. The shower at the YWCA was definitely worth the walk into town, even though I didn't make contact with Minneapolis. The rest of the crew is watching movies on the VCR and Eben has gone to Boston but will be back in the morning.

May 15

This is quite an experience so far! Today was spent working on the rigging again. It was a beautiful day and I can't think of any place I would rather be right now. My hands are sore but that should start working out pretty soon. The sun was out and a breeze is blowing out of the south that is cool if you get out of the sun. Two men with easels are up on the dock, painting pictures of the ship; they are from the artist colony across the harbor at Rocky Neck. Fishing boats are going in and out and lots of people walk out on the dock to talk and look at the boat. I like being on board working and not one of the lookers!

We removed the life rafts from the deck this morning by using a block and tackle and lowered them to the dock. They will be loaded into Eben's van and he'll take them to Boston for inspection.

May 16

The sun is hot and bright again today so I put on a sweatshirt; I got too much sun yesterday and burned my forearms. When the tide goes out we are way down below the dock and can't see anything but the pilings and junk. It gets very warm down here, but when the tide comes in we ride up until we are above the dock and the breeze starts hitting us again and we can see out into the Atlantic. There is a row of buoys leading out to sea, past an island with a light house .A very inviting view that I'm looking forward to being in, not looking at!

The cooking on this boat is fantastic! I guess they are trying out new things to feed the paying passengers this summer and meanwhile we are eating very well. Last night we had a dish with the big lobsters from the Theresa Marie, plus some scallops sauteed in wine with crackers and seasonings - excellent.

I finished the parceling and serving that we were going to do this morning, and after lunch I tackled the turnbuckles. Everything on this boat is so huge; some of the lines are big enough to move a barn and the tackle is very heavy duty. This afternoon we put the four main turnbuckles back on the chain plates and tightened them down. A welder was here to build up the chain plates where they have worn. The holes where the turnbuckles fit into the chain plates get a lot of wear and had elongated to a point where it was time to have them reinforced.

Again I'm covered with tar and silver paint and also sunburned. We left off a little early so we could clean up the deck and everything looks pretty neat until tomorrow when we start all over again.

George and Chris, two of the crew, are getting one of the "white hulls" in the water to see if they can get it to sail. It has a "spit" rig and they are trying to find all the rigging. It's a beautiful evening with just enough wind.

May 17, Friday

After dinner, I drove up along the shore (my car sounds very rough) and it is beautiful! Huge stone houses with stone fences around big wide green lawns, overlooking the harbor and ocean. I stopped to take a picture of a particularly pretty one and a guy on a bike stopped and came back wanting to know if I was really from Minnesota as my car license said. Turns out he is originally from Delano, Minnesota, and has been out here for eight years. We talked for a while and he told me of some interesting places to visit. I did find the beach he recommended, but there was no place to park the car, so I came back to the boat. George and Chris were sailing along across the harbor. I went to lie down for a while and slept all night. I must have been really tired!

Mary Ellen and Dave have gone to Maine for the weekend and will be back on Sunday night. Dan is the sole cook now for two days. He and Dave have been feuding and now Dan has the galley all to himself for the weekend, so it should be more peaceful down there. We keep getting fresh fish from the boats coming in, and for lunch today we had some monk fish that was excellent. It's a homely fish, so the first guy that ate it must have been awfully hungry, but it sure is good eating. They also gave us some squid that looks terrible, and I won't eat it, but Rich is very pleased, says it's a delicacy, and is going to take some home to eat.

Tomorrow is Saturday and I am going to run up to Rob's with some of the spare gear I brought and sort through my stuff some more and see what else I can leave behind.

May 20, Monday

Today much of the same thing: Art and I are still working on turnbuckles. We check for wear while trying to take them apart. Some of them are really frozen and it takes a lot of soaking in "kroil" (a mix of kerosene and oil) and a couple of huge pipe wrenches and hammers to loosen them up. We have to work them until they move smoothly.

We had a marine surveyor here all day, tapping and poking his sharp knife everywhere. He has pages of notes and as there are small pockets of dry rot everywhere he has dug into them and left little holes strewn behind him, like a squirrel looking for acorns in the yard. He is very thorough and has tapped his way all around the topsides in his little "pea pod," a double-ended boat he uses for a dingy. When he finishes the hull above the water line and on deck he will go aloft to check the rigging.

The rumor is that the boat is being sold to a man from Maine, and there is a lot of speculation about what will happen if the deal goes through. Will we all be out of a job before we even get a chance to sail on her?

We have a new crew member today: Ruth came on board this morning and now I am no longer the newest member of the crew.

May 21, Tuesday

More rigging work: rust busting and priming. I'm getting pretty proficient with the serving mallet. This is a long handled tool for putting the marlin wraps on the shrouds. It has a spool that holds the line and as you pass it around the shroud it lays the line smooth and tight - if you do it right! Clear and cold tonight. The gentleman from Maine that is looking to buy the *Gamage* was on board all day working with the surveyor.

May 22, Wednesday

Eben showed up this morning with the materials needed to finish the turnbuckles so we can get the rig back together. We took four more of the turnbuckles off to clean and grease them, and we're getting pretty speedy at this operation.

After lunch we got underway and rode out into the ocean so the surveyor could check the engine. I feel a little silly getting so excited about finally getting past the harbor entrance but I looked for dolphins and whales even though I knew we were too close to shore. I didn't want to turn around and come back in.

Tomorrow we cross over to the other side of the harbor to put the ship up on the ways so the bottom can be cleaned and painted. Both the surveyor and the Coast Guard will be there to check her out for soundness.

May 23, Thursday

Early call today. By 0600 we had breakfast out of the way and were underway for the other side of the harbor. We maneuvered between two piers and passed lines across to the men waiting on the docks. These bow lines were tied off and slowly a sled mounted on rails slid under the hull. We were secured to this and as the chain controlling the sled tightened we got pulled up and out of the water while the dock workers placed wedges under the hull at spaced intervals to keep us from falling over. It's a fascinating process, and a weird feeling to watch these two sliding docks move down towards us without any sense of movement. Actually I think we moved up into them, but whichever way, it was very slow and smooth until we were way up in the air and the keel of the *Gamage* was out of the water.

We are now sitting about 60 feet above the ground and have a beautiful view of the whole harbor and the town of Gloucester. When I stand here on the deck I can see across to where we were tied before and can almost see my car. I'll have to get a ride over there to get it over here.

To get down to the ground from here we have a very long wobbly metal ladder that is lashed to the side of the ship. The bottom of the ladder rests on the dock which is another eight or ten feet above the bottom of the harbor. Sometimes there is water under the dock but when the tide goes out it's dry.

To use the bathroom and showers we have to climb down the ladder and go across an open area to a large building full of equipment: Welders, cranes, big stacks of lumber, and other pieces of machinery lurk in the shadows. The lighting is very dim after the big doors are closed for the night and it's a real test of nerve to make the trip through all this and up a flight of stairs to the showers. The men that work here were considerate enough to remove most of the "girly" pictures that were on the walls the day after they knew there were three women that would be here for the yard period. I wonder if they were as uneasy about us being here as I was. I try to be out of there before everyone shows up for work or wait until after everyone leaves; with all the workers around it's kind of like walking through a men's locker room.

This seems to be a pretty big shipyard. Just on our left is a big steel tugboat. The tug is also clean out of the water and I never realized just how huge they are. They always look so short, stubby, and close to the water when they are out working in the river or harbor but actually they are kind of like an iceberg in that three quarters of them are underwater. The hull is magnificent and powerful looking. The welders are working back by the stern and there are large patches on the hull they have sanded and primed, and are now ready to paint.

Mary Ellen and I went exploring tonight and drove out towards the ocean; all the way out to the light house on the point at the entrance of the harbor. On the way back to the ship we stopped off at the "Rudder," a quaint little bar and restaurant, and were enjoying the atmosphere and the conversation when the rest of the crew dropped in. I can't believe that I am actually here, sitting in a dock side restaurant, right at the water's edge in Gloucester, Massachusetts. I'm part of the crew on a 100-ton gaff-rigged schooner that is about to embark on some unknown adventures.

At this time we have two Captains: Rich, who brought the ship up from the Virgin Islands after driving her down there all winter, and Art, who was supposed to relieve Rich but decided he would feel more comfortable being mate until he learned the schooner better. There's two cooks, Dan and Dave, who bunk in the same cabin and can't stand each other. Six crew: Mary Ellen and Sam, who have been aboard with Rich for the last season but are leaving right after the yard period; George, who signed on for the trip north from the Islands but has decided to stay on as crew; then Ruth, Chris, and I who have all just lately joined.

May 24, Friday

These ship yards don't waste any time. I woke up bright and early to the yard workers pounding on the hull. Right after breakfast we all went back to work, too. Art and I finally got the shrouds back together but we still have another coat of silver rust sealer to paint on the turnbuckles and shear pins. We'll have to wait to secure them until Eben shows up with the cotter pins.

Chris was here again today and it sounds like the Harvey is sold. Anyway the summer schedule will go on as planned so I will stay on the boat until fall - after that who knows?

Everyone had a beer on the deck after work tonight as it was very hot. Afterwards we all went to the bar and had a round. Then a "mystery" man bought every one another round. We couldn't figure out who it was and the bartender wouldn't tell us. We still don't know who that was.

After Art wandered in for the third time after trying and failing to find his way back to the boat, I decided to wrap it up and walk him home myself. There are still four of the crew sitting at the bar but I'm sure they can take care of themselves. The bar reminded me of the fancy dockside bars on Lake Minnetonka back home, where big boats come and tie up for a weekend of drinking and partying. The boats tied here at the bar pier are big private cruising boats from Boston, Marblehead, Salem and other towns along this coast that have come to Gloucester for a weekend of festivities.

May 25, Saturday

We worked till noon today and then had the afternoon off. As I have the only means of transportation I volunteered to use my car and do the wash this morning. Everyone handed up their dirty clothes and it took me from 8:30 till noon to get it all done. The gal at the laundromat told me to put a bottle of classic coke in with the detergent for the really greasy and dirty jeans; it's what the fisherman use to clean their work clothes. I tried it and it worked! She said the economy is terrible here in Gloucester; it looks okay to me but that's the gossip from the laundromat.

After lunch Mary Ellen, Ruth, and Chris wanted to pick up some foul weather gear, and George wanted a ride to the train stop as he is going to Boston for the weekend. We needed to get some supplies for Memorial Day, too. We got in my car, and dropped George off at the corner where the train picks you up off the street, just like waiting for a bus going down town. Ruth and Chris found some rain gear at the ship's store, then we made a stop at the A&P to pick up film and ice, then to the liquor store for the beer and vodka. The whole crew has pitched in for the beach party tomorrow.

We got back to the boat just in time to get the mattresses and pillows stowed below before a front came through with lots of thunder, lightning and heavy winds. We don't get too many chances to air out the beds so every opportunity we have, like this morning when it was hot and sunny, we like to bring some of it up on deck and air it out. The storm made us put everything below too soon but the rain did cool the air down and it feels good. I was a little apprehensive about being up so high out of the water in all the wind but we didn't even quiver. There are a few leaks in the deck when it rains this hard but none right over my bunk, so I stayed dry in my cabin; in some places it drips on the bunks and can get a little uncomfortable to say the least.

May 27, Monday - Memorial Day

At the crack of dawn this morning, as I was heading for the showers up in the men's locker room, I ran into Art pacing the decks with a frustrated look on his face. He had always gone up to Dunkin' Donuts in the morning for coffee when we were on the other side of the harbor but here there was no place to get any coffee this early. After I came back from the shower he was still there looking a little frantic for a caffeine and sugar fix so we took the *Eagle* (the ship's dingy) and made a run to town for coffee and donuts. It was well worth the time and the trip just for the conversation. It seems the ship that Art owned for 25 years, the brigantine *Romance*, was the ship used in the movie *Hawaii*, and after they finished with the movie it was put on the market and Art bought it. She was sold with all the groceries still on board and was well fitted for cruising. He sailed her twice around the world and chartered her out in the Caribbean for years. They just sold her last year. He has signed on to be the Captain for this trip and there should be more interesting stories coming up.

May 28, Tuesday

Pretty much the same yard stuff today. The shipyard crew is back at work after the holiday and they were pounding on the hull at 0700. I drove Dan to the Grocery store for some supplies and bought a pewter Ancient Mariner from the gift shop. Ruth and I worked on blocks all afternoon. Each block has to be taken apart, cleaned and checked, greased and then put back together. It's a slow job, and will probably keep us occupied for a couple of days as there are lots of them in the rigging.

Dave the cook is back and we had a great spaghetti dinner. Charlie is up on deck playing the guitar and it has cooled down some with a nice breeze.

We are still way up in the air on the "ways" and everything is covered with a fine, black, gritty sand from the sand blasting they are doing on the hull. It is a very efficient way of cleaning the hull but it sure is messy.

I've found that if I wait till the evening whistle blows and the yards close for the night, it's a much better time to take a shower. When I came back from the showers tonight I could hear voices but couldn't see any one - Charlie and Chris were way up in the rigging checking everything out. When Sam came back he went up too and they made the boat move with their climbing around.

May 29, Wednesday

We did blocks all day again today. Dave made donuts this morning and they were excellent. Eben showed up and made out the payroll. It was very hot until around 4:30 when it clouded up and poured like crazy again. Dan, Ruth and I went down to the Studio, a bar right on the water, but the mosquitoes were terrible so we moved into the piano bar. No player tonight as it's the middle of the week and there is no one here except us. We had a good visit and when Ruth and I decided to head back to the boat, Dan wandered off on his own. Chris stayed on the boat tonight and Mary Ellen was going to join us but never showed up. Sam, Charlie and Dave are off somewhere else. I'm sunburned and stiff so will get a good night's sleep and be ready for tomorrow.

May 30, Thursday

They are caulking the hull now, so when the seven a.m. whistle sounds the workers start pounding and tapping on the hull. They use a heavy mallet and it sounds like they are hitting the hull with a sledge hammer, but the ship is so solid that you can't feel anything - just hear the noise.

There was more sandblasting this morning and what a mess: black grit all over everything again. We swept and vacuumed the deck after they were through but it settles everywhere. When we get back in the water we will have to take the fire hose and hose it all down. That's one of the many nice things about a boat: when you get a mess like this you can just turn the water on it and wash it off.

One coat of primer was sprayed on the hull this afternoon but it looks like it will take a lot more coats before it starts to cover.

We are almost done with the blocks we can reach and today Chris and Art went to the top of the rigging and dropped down the big triple blocks for the main throat halyard. They must weigh at least 35 pounds each, and after we took one all apart and greased it, we sent it back up on a line. The next interesting job is to restring the halyards through all those pulleys.

There is a whole different culture on these boats. Everyone on board seems to have lots of family and friends but no one seems to own anything that really ties them to the land. They talk of cars stashed in different places and storage places for extra possessions; though no one seems to have much in the way of worldly possessions or even cash to call their own. The ones that have been on board different ships for a while talk of places like Argentina, Madagascar, Australia and so on as if it was a place right next door. They go from one tall ship to another depending on where a ship is going and if that's where they want to go or not. It is a very close knit, small world, where everyone seems to know everyone else on the other ships and all the news and gossip through the very efficient grapevine.

It's now official: Art Kimerly, the ex-owner of the *Romance*, will be the Captain, and Rich, the Captain that brought the boat up from the south, will be the first mate. I guess Rich was planning to take a different job on a smaller ship that paid more money, so Eben hired Art as Captain. Then the job that Rich was going to take didn't jell, so he's come back on the Harvey as first mate. At least that's the story we are hearing right now. I'm glad and rather relieved about this as Art really isn't familiar with a schooner and hasn't sailed the Maine coast, whereas Rich has sailed this boat for a couple of years and he grew up here and learned to sail in these waters.

June 3, Monday

Did the ships' laundry and took Dan over for groceries and ice. Ruth hitched a ride to the train stop and from there I drove up to Rob's for the evening. I spent Saturday night and Sunday there and we made some garage sales. I got an old bentwood rocker for $3 and a picture of an oak tree in a field. We barbecued on Sunday night and on Monday morning at 7:15 Rob dropped me off and took my car to work. We will be sailing soon and this was the last chance I had to get the car to Rob's for storage. It's kind of a lonesome feeling. I talked to Jon and Gary *(her sons)* Sunday afternoon to say I'd be sailing this week.

We sanded, brushed, and sponged the top sides of the Harvey. Everyone was hanging over the rails by their toe nails, or standing on the scaffolding and reaching up. At around two p.m. Eben showed up with the white paint and the whole crew went to work painting the topsides. At six we stopped for dinner and then went right back at it until around eight p.m. when it started to rain.

June 4, Tuesday

I don't think the pork chops we had for dinner yesterday agreed with me. I threw them up and then slept all night. What a night! This yard is not the place to feel sick, especially in the middle of the night, and it's not the place you want to be when you're not feeling well at any time. When you have to use a bathroom in the middle of the night when we're way up in dry dock like this it's quite a feat. First you have to climb up on deck from your cabin. The way to the deck is down a hallway with a very dim light and up a 10-foot ladder. Now you cross the deck and climb up on a box or can to step across the cap rail unto another ladder. Then down the 60-foot metal ladder on the outside of the hull to the dock, then up the dock and across the parking lot to the ship yard shed. There is a key for the unlocking door to the shed. Now the best part: The shed, which is at least 300 feet long, is dark except for one dim light back in a corner, and full of big spooky machinery and paint cans. You have to walk the whole length of the shed to a flight of stairs which winds up and into the men's locker room where the door closes but doesn't lock. The imagination can get very active in here: It's dark and scary, and every little noise sounds dangerous. It's also pouring rain with thunder and lightning. Then of course you have to backtrack through the whole thing in order to get back to your bunk.

Today we are going back in the water! We sail Saturday for Boston and my son Rob and grandson Greg are coming along for the ride. It's raining buckets of cold rain and very windy out of the north. I broke out the Henri Lloyds *(a brand of sailing clothes)* after wearing the lighter set of rain gear and freezing. This morning I spent four and a half hours washing and folding the ships' laundry: 65 sheets and all the towels and pillow cases that go with them - 20 tubs of clothes. I thought I could put the stuff in the tubs and do some cross stitching - forget that! By the time I got everything sorted and loaded in the tubs it was time to take the first loads out and start the drying and folding process.

When I got back to the ship everyone seemed to have disappeared but they were all below decks working on different projects. Next we have to get the forecastle cleaned up and ready for the crew. When this is done the crew will move out of the passenger cabins and then we can clean and make them up for the weekend: We pick up 22 passengers in Boston on Sunday, going to Bar Harbor.

June 5, Wednesday

Still up on the ways. Miserable cold rain. We polished brass and cleaned. I feel like we will be here forever. I walked to the mailbox to mail some letters and still have an upset stomach. The stove is being fixed so we had pizza delivered for dinner.

June 6, Thursday

At 6 a.m. this morning we started to slide back down the ramp and into the water. The whole crew was on deck and all the guys from the shipyard were standing by on the docks as we slipped backwards. It took about 15 minutes before we were clear of the ramp and were actually floating again. They cranked the big blocks out from under the hull and we were free to go.

Sam was below decks, with a flashlight, checking all the through hull for leaks. When he reported that all was dry, the engine was started and as we backed out from between the docks, all the lines were pulled in and coiled. Just as we were turned and headed out to the harbor for a clean shot across to the other side, the engine died! There was a pretty stiff breeze blowing us back down the bay into a fleet of anchored boats and it looked like we would wipe the whole bunch out.

Rich ordered the anchor dropped and it didn't take but a few minutes before we had a 350-pound anchor and chain over the side. With the anchor down and holding, we started to swing across the anchor line of a small (30 foot) sailboat. It looked like we might ride right over her. The only thing we could see to do was walk her around our bowsprit before she got tangled and pushed under by our sheer weight.

When her shrouds got close to our main shrouds Art and Chris boarded her. They held her away from our rigging and hull and we didn't touch. Some of the crew crawled out to the end of the bowsprit to help walk her around. Then we put an extension on her painter as the short mooring line the owners had her on wasn't long enough to reach all the way around to the windward side of us.

After we had settled down on the hook and knew we wouldn't be running into any more boats, and the little sailboat was riding very nicely about ten feet away on our windward side, they went to check the engine. We must have motored over to the boat yard on fumes last week because we are out of fuel. The last time the boat had taken on any fuel was in Bermuda.

Ten gallons of diesel from the emergency supply was dumped into the tank and Charlie took off in the whitehull to row across the harbor for help. The whitehulls are little boats we carry on davits all the time, and are used for sailing and rowing in the harbor. Eben had been on the dock waiting for us to come across in the *Gamage*, wondering what was going on. He came back with Charlie and helped get the engine started.

When the engine was running smoothly we raised the anchor. What a job. Two of the crew get on a big windlass and crank the anchor up a few links at a time. When the anchor ring is above the water a hook on a heavy line is passed over the side to snag the ring in the top of the anchor and then the anchor is attached to a block and tackle. This is called the" anchor burton," and has two big double blocks that are attached high on the rig to lift that 350-pound anchor. It takes two more crew members to raise the anchor up with the burton until it is high enough to bring aboard and secure to the rail.

We made it across the bay without any more problems and tied up at the fuel dock. As we started taking on water, a fuel barge flying a red bravo flag rafted up on the outside and started pumping diesel into our tanks. Filling the diesel tanks takes a while and there were two fishing boats impatiently waiting to get to the dock. The decision was made to cast us off from the dock to drift in the harbor, still attached to the fuel barge pumping diesel into our tanks. The fishing boats moved in around us. There were all these huge ships and trawlers maneuvering around us, jockeying for position, but nobody bumped anyone else and we finally finished fueling and got back to our old dock.

The only spot open for us was to tie up alongside another big trawler. This makes things a little more difficult as we need to carry all the stuff from the deck that Eben wants to take back with him, and load it in his van. After all this is done it's only eight a.m.!

At 0800 the Coast Guard was due on board for the annual safety inspection. We had all the life jackets spread on the deck for him to check, and he had a whole list of other things that had to be checked off.

After two hours of this we finally got to go sailing! We are actually going out on the ocean. I've been looking out past the harbor entrance for three weeks now, wishing we could go out there and now we will.

The sun is shining and the wind is blowing as we head out into the harbor and turn the bow into the channel between the red and green buoys. There is an old abandoned light house on an island that is very picturesque; it would make a good place for a summer cabin. When we pass the breakwater light that I walked out to last week I thought that I'd much rather see it from this perspective than standing on shore. Off to our starboard is a huge structure that stands out in the middle of nowhere. It's a platform that had been used for setting up the town's sewage system but caught fire and was abandoned. It looks like a big spider. I'd hate to run into it on a dark night.

As we finally head out into the north Atlantic some huge leftover swells lift the boat gently up and over. This is great! The ship feels like it's coming alive under my feet!

The mainsail, foresail, and staysail are raised. It takes a lot of muscle to get these huge gaff sails up. We have four crew on each side of the boat, one team at the main throat halyard and the other team on the peak halyard. Once the main is up everyone moves forward and does the same thing with the fore. The staysail doesn't take as much muscle but it still takes four crew.

This is really spectacular and beautiful; the masts are so tall and there is such an expanse of sail and intricate rigging that I'm completely fascinated and love to just look up at it. I wish I could get a picture of the whole process but it is in my head so that will have to do for now.

The lister, a diesel engine used for pumping water and charging batteries, is started up for the Coast Guard's check off. We are shooting a powerful stream of salt water out of the fire hose and as long as it's running we get brushes, buckets of salt water and "Joy" to wash all that black dust from the sandblasting into the ocean.

The CG inspector climbs all the way up in the rigging to check it out, and when he's back on deck we tack.

We are under sail only; the engine has been shut down. This is a heavy displacement ship and not real quick to maneuver, so the tack takes a long time, especially in this light wind. We back the jib, sheet in the main, and hold the helm hard over. It was a slow process but we didn't use the engine and finally filled the jib from the other side and headed back to the dock. I really don't want to turn around!

As we enter the harbor under power, we drop and furl these huge sails. It's unbelievable the size and weight of the lines, blocks and tackle used to run this boat. I'm sure there are boats with heavier equipment than this, but for me this is such a big step up from a yacht.

After tying up and getting everything stowed and looking shipshape, we have Chinese takeout for dinner. The stove is still being bricked so we can't cook anything. Not even coffee for breakfast. Art is very happy that we are back on the Gloucester side of the harbor and have the Dunkin' Donuts close by so he can get his caffeine fix in the morning.

Dave has picked up a movie - "Carousel" - and we all watched it after dinner. Everyone is tired, even the young guys. It has been a very long, hard day.

I couldn't have been asleep long when I woke to the sound of water gurgling against the hull! It was the whine of turning screws, churning the water right next to my ear. I was wide awake instantly and all the sudden yelling up on deck spurred me on.

When I got on deck I saw a large fishing boat backing into the very narrow space between us and the next dock! The noise had roused most of our crew so we stood by with fenders. The Captain of the trawler did an excellent job and never touched us, though the tender almost got scrunched between us and the *Theresa Marie*, but George caught it in time and moved it around the other side.

This has been a very exciting day and I actually sailed on this boat today. Tomorrow we do some more cleaning below decks and Saturday we leave for Boston!

June 7, Friday
0430

It's still dark but the fishing boat we are rafted to wants to leave to go fishing. We had rafted to the outside of him last evening so he is between us and the dock and we have to let him out and then re-tie all the lines.

Once we got settled down again, the *Theresa Marie*, on our other side, starts taking on ice from a noisy metal chute. There is lots of shouting and banging as they take on supplies for their fishing trip.

By this time there is no going back to sleep, but the sun is up and shining and it looks like a beautiful day. We have planned on washing blankets today and although it is pretty chilly now, it will warm up. The stove is still being bricked and it must get very expensive feeding this crew with takeout food. I know the pizza was $50 and the Chinese must have been at least $90 with all the extra stuff. Now we are getting Dunkin' Donuts and coffee for breakfast. I think we'll just air the blankets out and save the washing for some other time when the expenses aren't so high.

I hate to even think what the yard period must have cost. And with the CG inspection over we have to replace all 12 of the expired parachute flares, plus all the orange smoke flares and 18 of the life jackets. None of this is cheap and there are lots of other expenses too. I guess fresh washed blankets are not high on the priority list. Instead I spent all morning until 1:30 this afternoon washing and folding sheets and some of the light blue cotton blankets, plus the crew laundry.

Mary Ellen has moved out of the cabin that she has been in for a year. It is right off the saloon and as she is leaving soon, Ruth and I are moving in there together. We cleaned the cabin and moved all our stuff in. Next we had to clean all the cabins the crew had been using and make them up with clean sheets, blankets and towels for the friends and family that will be sailing to Boston with us tomorrow.

First Voyages

June 8, Saturday

Rob, Greg, and Greg's friend Wayne showed up at 7:30 this morning for the sail to Boston. It is a beautiful sunny day and the wind couldn't be better.

When everyone was on board and breakfast out of the way we got ready to leave. Rich, who is now the Captain again, decides to sail off the dock -- right from downtown Gloucester. He gives the command for the mainsail to be raised. With four people on each side -- four on the throat and four on the peak halyards, the main sail is raised and secured. We cast off and start slipping back away from the dock. The command for the staysail to be raised and backed is given. With two people on the halyard, one on the outhaul, and two on the sheet, the staysail is hauled up and backed. The wind caught it on the starboard side and forced the bow of the boat to port and out into the channel, headed toward the harbor entrance. Once we are making way the command is given to raise the foresail and jib. We repeat the process used for raising the main and staysail and soon we are sailing out of Gloucester harbor under full sail! I think the Captain was showing off a little; it was very impressive and spectacular. Everything went smoothly and the wind couldn't have been better for the maneuver. I guess when you think of it, this was the only way to get out of here for these big schooners before they had engines. Either sail out or have their yawl boats push them.

Rob pitched right in and helped raise sails. He took Greg out on the bowsprit after we were underway, and one of the foot ropes broke under him. Rich was a little nervous about having the ropes break under a "Coastie" even if he is my son, but Rob didn't say anything. He really didn't have to! Luckily he didn't have both feet on one line and was hanging on, so he didn't fall through, but replacing the bad spots in the net has suddenly gone to the top of the list of things to do. Then Greg went all the way to the top of the mast spreaders.

We had a great sail and pulled into Pier 7 in Boston around 2:30. Rob, Greg and Wayne took a cab to the CG station and then will catch the 5:30 train back to Gloucester where they left the car. Everyone else off boarded and then most of the crew went out to explore the town. Art, Mary Ellen and I stayed on board and finally crashed about 11 p.m. A storm threatened with lots of big black clouds, thunder, and lightning, but it passed just south of us and we didn't get a drop.

June 9, Sunday

Mary Ellen has left for her bus ride of 3500 miles to visit family and friends in Texas and California. Ruth, Charlie and I have cleaned and made up most of the cabins while everyone else left for church and such. It's now 2:30 and they aren't back, and I'm getting a little worried about the heads and the other cabins that the crew had guests in and had promised to clean. But if we start doing the scrub lady bit this early in the season, there will be no way out, and it will expected of us. As much as I'd like to get everything shipshape for the passengers boarding tonight, I've been advised to hold off and let the rest of the crew finish what they had promised to do when they get back on board. So Ruth and I walked over to Atlantic Avenue and brought back some fish sandwiches which we shared with Art and Eben on the deck house roof. Eben and Art had finally found the air leak in the lister pump and it is pumping and holding its prime.

The crew showed up and all the cabins got cleaned and all four heads are cleaned and working. I guess I shouldn't worry so much.

We boarded 22 high school students, all wearing red T-shirts with a picture of the *Harvey Gamage* on them. They will be studying whales, seals and dolphins with three teachers they brought with them. We are also expecting a naturalist from the College of the Atlantic in Bar Harbor.

The *Spirit of Massachusetts* came into port led by a fire boat shooting water up from about ten hoses. She was under full sail and looked spectacular! Our whole crew was invited to a party on her but I don't really feel like going. Art and Eben went and some of the crew but I'm going to bed. It's been another long day and tomorrow we leave for "down east," stopping at Gloucester tomorrow night.

2200

Just before I went below to crash, a boat came along side and hailed us. He was alone, pretty drunk, and needed help landing his boat at the dock. I went down and caught a line to pull the boat in. We got it all secure and talked for a while. He lives in Boston but takes his boat the *Sea Hog* to the Bahamas every fall. As he wouldn't be back to the boat till next weekend he gave me all the stuff out of his cooler: barbecue chicken wings and Greek salad.

June 10, Monday

There are jelly fish all over the harbor. They are called moon jellies and are very pretty as they pulsate through the water, but I definitely would not want to go swimming. Dave claims they are harmless but are not very nice to come in contact with as they have the consistency of cold slimy egg white.

We left Boston at 9 a.m. and had a beautiful sail out to Stellwaggon Banks where we saw lots of whales. They weren't very close and since we were a little slow under sail, rather than start the engine we just drifted. Rich says the whales like the big sailing ships and usually come over to us, but they were busy eating I guess and without much wind we didn't have any luck chasing them. I did get some pictures of black dots on the water.

The sail into Gloucester was great but we did a sloppy job dropping the sails. We were off the wind running into the harbor as we tried to drop the sails and they kept getting caught in the lazy jacks.

I'm not quite sure why we didn't head up to drop them but there must have been a good reason. They did get stowed finally and now we are tied up again in the same place we left two days ago. Dan is cooking fish and we will watch "Captains Courageous" tonight with the high school kids.

June 11, Tuesday

 We left Gloucester at eight a.m. this morning and headed back to the banks for more whale watching. When we left the harbor it was cold and damp without much wind, but as we cleared the entrance the wind picked up and the damp turned into a haze that made the land disappear very quickly. The sun shone where we were even though we couldn't see the shore. The sailing was beautiful for about two hours, and we used this time to get the daily chores out of the way. The deck was hosed down with salt water and the cap rails and deck house were wiped down with fresh water and special colored sponges, used just for fresh water. There is constant maintenance on a ship and one this size keeps everyone busy all the time.

The Captain spent some time today getting the crew together and helping us understand how he wants things done. This will really help because until now there has been at least six different ways to do one thing, and the person watching always had a different way. Now it's understood which way is the "right" way for this Captain. That will probably change with the next Captain, but for now we should be able to work together without too much controversy.

We saw lots of whales and they are spectacular! First we would see a "blow" of white spray on the surface as they came up from below, then the back and fin would curl out of the water and finally the flukes. If they hump their backs and flip the whole fluke up, that usually means they will dive deep and not be back up for about 15 minutes. We would see six and seven of them at a time and stayed out to watch them until around 3 p.m.

We came back to Gloucester for the night and decided to take advantage of the showers and laundromat. We can't seem to get away from here. When we came out of the YWCA we walked into a wild storm with pouring rain, thunder, lightning, wild winds, and hail.

A fishing boat pulled in after dark and rafted next to us with the whole cockpit filled to the gunwales with bait fish. Mixed in with the herring were some weird looking sea creatures; some looked like worms, and others I didn't recognize at all. The sea gulls had a feast, sitting on the pile of fish to pick out the little juicy tidbits that would work up to the top.

June 12, Wednesday

We glided silently and majestically out of Gloucester harbor this morning at 0800 in an almost fog, a very thick haze with about a half-mile visibility. Other boats ghosted out of the haze and then disappeared. Once clear of the harbor we took departure bearings from the R2 buoy off Thatcher Island on a heading of 050. We will be sailing all night so we laid out a DR (dead reckoning) track and the crew has been split into watches. Rich, Ruth and I are on the first watch from 0800 to 1200.

After lunch I was going to try a celestial shot and found the watch I'd been using has died. Then I couldn't get a time tick on my radio. But the horizon is very hazy so the shot wouldn't have been accurate anyway. It's a good thing I brought the equipment out though, because now I know I'll need new batteries before anything will work. Much better to find this out now!

At 1600 all sails were dropped and secured for a storm coming through. Everyone put on foul weather gear and it was quite a fashion show with all the new stuff. We watched the storm on the radar and could see it approaching. When it should have hit us it just kind of dissipated with a little rain and some lightning. There are still big black blobs of storms showing on the radar so we are motoring and staying on storm watch.

1700

We are in the middle of a great storm, with simultaneous lightning and thunder. Rich had cleared the decks of all but a few crew and I was at the helm when a tremendous blast of lightning shot right over our heads. Everyone flinched and now only Rich and Charlie are on deck as I've been sent below also. I'd rather be up there. Though there is a lot of wind and rain there's not much in the way of seas as we had a wind shift to the NW and there hasn't been time for seas to build.

June 13, Thursday

The storm blew over but it still rained pretty solidly for a while. Our watch was relieved at 2000 and as I didn't plan the trip down at dinner time to get something to eat, it was all gone by the time I got there. I fooled around with the charts for a while and then crawled into bed, curled up in a ball and went right to sleep. I slept like a log until 0330 when we got up for the 0400 - 0800 watch. What a beautiful morning. We are sailing under foresail only and cruising along some of the most seaward islands off the Maine coast. We saw some puffins, razorback ducks, and a few seals. The wind is out of the NW and very cold with lots of whitecaps. The water here is the same grey color as Lake Superior, not the pretty cobalt blue of the waters further south. That must have something to do with the temperature of the water.

The wind keeps building and it's starting to get a little interesting. This boat (Art says it's a SHIP, not a boat), at 95 feet is very solid and with the masts raked back there is very little heel. We have taken the main and the foresails down because the wind was getting a little stiff and we are sailing under staysail only. It is cold and rainy but we should be at Burnt Coat Cove around 1230.

2200

Supper is out of the way and Ruth and I had the dishes tonight. Rich asked me to take a watch this afternoon so he could get some rest and all the kids went ashore to explore. About 1500 a squall went through and we started to drag anchor fast! I woke Rich up real quick and he started the engine and held our position until the wind died down. We must have dragged at least 10 boat lengths before everything was under control again; the shore behind us was only about a boat length away. Fortunately we were still in the channel as it runs close to shore on this side. The squall passed over and the sun came out. Rich thanked me for waking him up in time, looked around and went below. We will take turns at anchor watch all night tonight. The stars are fantastic.

June 14, Friday

We woke up to full sunshine and lots of wind. The anchor was really fouled after dragging it last night in that squall; it had wire cables, plastic bags and lots of other junk tangled in the flukes and all the way up the shank. I can see why they call this Burnt Coat Harbor because the mud on the anchor smelled just like an old burnt wool coat.

We had a beautiful sporty sail out to Mount Desert Rock. The wind was on a beam reach both ways and there were some left over swells that heaved us gently up and down. It couldn't have been better. As we approached Mt. Desert we could see a lot of harbor seals sunning themselves. It's deep right up to shore so we worked in close and got a good look at them. They look so serious with those huge brown eyes peering at us over their whiskers. They stayed pretty far away but once in a while one would pop up right next to the boat.

There are lobster pots all around and we managed to catch one in the prop as we wove our way carefully through. I watched off the stern until it broke loose and popped up behind us. I hope its line isn't tangled in the prop.

When we got back to the mainland we circled Little Duck Island but the tide was high so any seals that were around were swimming and spread out. We anchored at Isleport on Cranberry Island, and right after we got the hook set a boat with a man and two small boys came out to see us. They were so involved with waving and smiling that they didn't see a lobster pot buoy and they hit it, chewing it up and spitting out chunks of styrofoam from the marker. It killed the engine and cut the line so he had to unwind the line from his prop and put a temporary marker on the trap. Then they smiled, waved and left.

It's my turn for tender duty. Dave and Dan, and George and Peter from the College of the Atlantic, all wanted to go ashore. I took them in and walked to the store with them, past lovely old well-kept homes. Nice place, and a beautiful little bay.

I kept the tender away from the boat too long and found out, in no uncertain terms, that the tender is to come right back to the boat and not wait for passengers. The thing to do is set up a time for the return trip, go back to the boat and wait. Just in case the tender is needed for something else.

June 15, Saturday

Because we dragged anchor the other night and it's still a little windy tonight, Rich has set up an all night anchor watch. I drew the 0330 till 0500. There was a beautiful ruby red sunrise, illuminating the clouds as they slowly moved in to make it dark and overcast again, and then it started to drizzle. Not a ripple on the water, and I spotted a couple of seals swimming around, leaving a long wake behind them. Lots of birds. "Red sky at morning, sailors take warning"?

At 0500 I crawled into my bunk for a while and at 0700 it was raining and dead calm. The anchor came up clean, but boy what a lot of work! We were under way before breakfast and motored fairly close to shore in the calm. This country is magnificent! There are high rocky hills rising right out of the sea and hundreds of little islands scattered around the bays. We sailed around the tip of Mt. Desert Island and arrived in Bar Harbor around 0900.

After we pick up the anchor buoy in front of the College of the Atlantic the students will be off boarded with the tender. The dock on the shore in front of the college was built just for the *Harvey Gamage* but we can't use it at low tide as there isn't enough water. We could put the bow over the dock but you have to be very agile to climb through the head rig. The students will stay at the college next week for classroom study.

The three-masted schooner *Natalie Todd* left the dock in Bar Harbor, under power, with all her sails set. There is no wind but every day, wind or calm, rain or shine, twice a day, she takes passengers for a two hour sail. I think this would get old very soon, but she is a pretty boat with her white hull and red gaff rigged sails, and there is always a good crowd of people that want to take a ride. Some of the crew may get a chance to sail on her for a couple of days as the *Harvey* has been overbooked and in order to adhere to CG regulations we have to leave some people on shore.

Once the students were off we left the College anchor buoy and are now tied at the dock right next to downtown Bar Harbor. Ruth and I walked up town for a little while to look around. There is a lot to see and explore and I'm looking forward to spending more time browsing.

I have volunteered to stand watch tonight and everyone else has gone off to a party. This boat is quite an attraction and all kinds of people line the dock to look at her and take pictures. They can peek thought the portholes into the saloon where I'm writing and every once in a while I catch someone in the window peeking at me.

Art came back so we sat and talked until around 9:30 when Rich and Charlie came in. Now everything is quiet. Earlier tonight Eben gave some of us a ride up to the College of the Atlantic to take advantage of the offer of showers and laundry facilities. The showers are in a summer house that was built for John Joshua Ebenezer in the early 1900s. It is fabulous! There is a great view of Frenchman's Bay from the balconies that are on each floor and can be reached through the individual rooms. It is built out of huge granite blocks, three stories high, and looks like a castle. Old fashioned high ceilings, a beautiful staircase, and in each room a fireplace. Imagine having a fireplace and a balcony overlooking Frenchman's Bay in your bedroom.

All the bunks are cleaned and made up for the new group of passengers that will be boarding tomorrow at noon. Eben has taken the ships' laundry to have it done commercially, so the crew are on their own for clean clothes this week.

June 16, Sunday

Washed my clothes this morning. It's overcast and at 1130 we boarded 26 4H kids with four leaders that will be on board for just three days. We sailed at 2:30 in pea soup fog and got to Isleford just in time to get the anchor set before it started to pour rain. There is some heated discussion going on about the watch schedule. It seems that whoever is making it out isn't rotating the time slots well enough to please everyone. It's very cold and wet but it is supposed to clear off by tomorrow afternoon. We erected the big white canvas deck cover that is supposed to protect the main deck for the passengers. It is primarily a sun shield and in this rain it leaks pretty badly. We ate our dinner of fried chicken and rice in three shifts because it was too wet to eat on deck. What a nightmare come true -- 26 energetic young teenagers stuck on a 95-foot boat in pouring rain!!

I had the 0230 to 0400 watch again and it was pitch dark and pouring. There were a couple of lights on shore and one lighted buoy that could be used for reference as an anchor watch, but other than that nothing could be seen. The wind was squally out of the NE and the best protection was to sit in a companionway to avoid most of the wind and wet and still be able to check for dragging. A very interesting night.

June 17, Monday

Still raining and cold this morning; everything is wet and damp. Ben, the head leader, is trying to keep everyone occupied and has set up a series of learning stations in different parts of the boat. I have a marlinespike station and will be teaching knots.

0230

The fog lifted and the wind shifted around to the east. The weather station guaranteed sun for the afternoon and the day started to warm up. And after lunch the sun did come out and we wound our way through a series of beautiful rocky islands in Blue Hill Bay. We saw some harbor porpoise and lots of seals. There was even a loon yodeling at us for a while.

As we approached our chosen anchorage for the night I noticed another boat already there. I couldn't help thinking that they must not be too happy to see us pull in with a boat load of very noisy kids. Dave tried for the fourth time to light the cannon for the flag ceremony, but it just fizzles. That gun had better be cleaned and operated properly before someone gets hurt. They don't have the proper fuse and are using black powder rolled up in paper towels.

We took a bunch of people ashore to explore and found all kinds of sea urchins and shells. There are sea urchin shells way up in the woods where the birds carry them. The woods are very lush and thick and look like they have never been cut or burned. The underbrush is full of fallen trees and it makes walking very difficult. Once the sun went down, the mosquitoes became terrible!!

We got back to the boat as quickly as possible because of the swarms of bugs and the people that had to wait for rides in the tender would stand on shore looking like Indians doing a wild dance, jumping up and down and swatting mosquitoes.

I had the 1230 to 0200 watch and the stars were spectacular. With a flashlight I could see lots of moon jellies pulsating through the water and when I turned the light off there were "fireflies" glowing in amongst the jelly fish. Just before my watch was over the stars faded as fog and cloud cover moved in again.

June 18, Tuesday

It is still very cold. There was a Pan-Pan at 0200 this morning just as I was getting ready to fall asleep. There are two people in the water somewhere off Portsmouth. The CG is making the announcement on the radio and it sounds like the couple's boat sank and they got a message out but haven't been located yet. This is awful cold water to spend any time in.

The fog started to lift around 1000 so we pulled the anchor and headed out to open water. The sun is shining through the overcast in places lighting up large areas of beautiful blue water. Off in the distance an island top would show up through the fog and then we would sail into a wall of solid white where nothing except the immediate boat is visible. The fog horn sounding off every three minutes sounds ghostly and forlorn; it gives me an eerie feeling of foreboding. A power boat passed in front of us but he looked like a mirage floating way up in the sky.

Now the wind has started to blow warmer and the fog is lifting. There are islands and fish traps all around us again. When we spot the buoy marking the open ocean we head east to sail out to Mt. Desert Island, which is 20 miles off shore.

As we approach Mt. Desert Island there is another schooner, the *American Eagle,* off our port bow about five miles. I hope we get close enough to get some pictures. The fog completely burned off and we had a beautiful sail. I sure like it out here away from the land. After we sailed around the island for a while we headed back for the mainland and the plan is to anchor in Somes Sound tonight.

Somes Sound is the only fiord on the North American continent. It's a deep, narrow body of water that runs eight to ten miles inland from the coast of Mt. Desert Island. Some of the shoreline is sheer cliffs of rock rising straight out of the water; then there are stretches where the shore is gentle with homes and big estates along the waterfront. I think this is one of my favorite spots up here and the scenery is truly spectacular.

We fought a five-knot tidal current as we worked inland, but now we're anchored in a little cove with a couple of other boats. As I have the 1230 watch tonight there isn't much reason to go to bed. The sky is a little overcast but a few stars are peeking through and it's dead calm. Most of the kids are going for a hike in the morning so the boat is quiet.

June 19, Wednesday

This cove, where we are anchored, is at the bottom of a very steep cliff with a small sandy beach for a narrow foothold. From this beach there is a trail that leads to the summit. Sitting here on the steering box I have to lean back to see the top of the cliff. That should be quite a climb. I have decided to stay on board; there were enough bugs last night to last me for a while.

Floating alongside the boat was the ugliest mass of gunk I've ever seen, and it was alive! Everyone had gone ashore to hike up the cliff and I was looking down at the water just watching the tide run by, when I spotted this ugly jelly fish. It looked like a big red blood clot with long stringy tentacles streaming out behind the egg yolk colored film floating around it. The main body was as big as an ice cream bucket and it really looks gross! I have no idea if it's poisonous or not but I wouldn't want to be in the water with it. It hung out alongside the hull for a while and then drifted off with the current. When the naturalist came back from the hike I found out it's called a lion's mane.

The sun is bright this morning and the view from the top of the cliff should be spectacular. When the kids got up there though they saw a huge fog bank rolling in from the ocean so came back early. We got ready to get underway and I volunteered to go "in the hole." George claimed it wasn't his turn and Charley has been having a lot of trouble with the skin on his hands cracking.

When the anchor is "weighed" there is usually about 150 ft of anchor chain that has been run out. As the anchor is pulled up that chain is fed into the anchor locker, and someone has to be down there in the "hole" to guide it into place.

There are two sections for anchor chain in the bow of the boat. One side holds the port anchor chain and the other side holds the starboard chain. There isn't a partition between the two, and just enough room for the chain when it's all stowed properly. I had to back down feet first, and then push my rear end over to the other side of the chain locker to squat on the starboard anchor chain. As the anchor is raised and the chain comes into the locker I was to pick up about a two foot section by the links and lay it out neatly. It isn't a very hard job, but the quarters are a little cramped and by the time all that chain comes in off the bottom you get pretty messy with whatever the chain brings up from down there. Sometimes there is clay and sometimes mud, but whatever it is there is always rust.

By the time everything is secure and you are called out of the hole you are pretty messy. Whoever is on deck has a bucket of salt water and some Joy dish soap handy for you to wash all the mud and stuff off.

Surrounded by the thickest pea soup fog I've seen yet, we slowly motored back towards the sea. A couple of times we would hear engines and then a lobster boat would appear out of the fog, poke around working their traps for a while, and then disappear. The high hills on both sides of the sound would appear occasionally as dark smudges high in the air. I was on the bow giving signals to the helm so we could dodge the lobster buoys that would pop up almost under us. If we couldn't avoid them in time, I'd give the "cut" signal and the engine would be put in neutral so the prop wouldn't be as likely to catch and cut them.

We could hear the fishing boats way before we could see them and it made for a very interesting trip. When I'd hear something I'd signal back to Rich the direction of the sound and he could usually verify it on the radar. One time I heard an engine approaching and Rich couldn't see anything on radar but started sounding the fog horn. In about three minutes a plane flew out of the fog past our bow.

As we entered the Bar Harbor anchorage we couldn't see a thing. Large boats at anchor would materialize out of the mist almost close enough to touch. With Charley at the helm, Rich with his eyes glued to the radar giving directions, and two bow watches, Rich did a fantastic downwind landing that was faultless. Eben met us at the dock with all the clean laundry so we spent the next couple of hours cleaning cabins and making up the bunks for the next group of passengers.

1400

The next group of 4H kids is boarded and settled in and we will be departing shortly for another three day charter. It's still very foggy and cold but this will be just a short run to our first night's anchorage. The fog has started to lift and by the time we left the dock at 3 p.m. the sun was shining and we had a very brisk wind.

There seems to be a tradition among the Maine schooners that you have to have every sail up before leaving the harbor- especially if there is another schooner around. This is to "show off" for the people watching from shore. Main, fore and staysail were up and flying by the time we cleared the harbor entrance.

There was another schooner that left the same time we did so we had a race going. She tacked and crossed our stern but in doing so got between us and open water. We didn't have room to tack in front of her and the shore was getting closer all the time. Rich got on the radio and they worked out the close quarters maneuver. She tacked again and headed up into Frenchman's Bay and we tacked out to sea.

As we cleared the light on Egg Rock, the fog closed in again. Just like sailing into a wall. The radar is unbelievable. We sailed between buoys that we couldn't see until they were right there, and although we were only a half mile off shore, and could hear the surf on the rocks, we couldn't see any sign of the land.

In fog like this we move very slowly so it takes longer to get anywhere, but by 1900 we ghosted our way into Little Cranberry harbor and put the hook down in a little patch of clear air. The warmth from the land breeze must have chased the fog away in the harbor but as the sun went down we got socked in solid again.

Throwing a bucket of water into the calm harbor at night disturbs the plankton and they flash like blue fireflies where the splashing water stirs them up. It's a good way to pass time on a quiet midnight anchor watch.

June 20, Thursday

Finally we woke up to a clear sunny day. The wind was perfect to sail off the anchor. We cut around Little Duck Island and sailed out into the open ocean until noon.

What a beautiful day although it is rather chilly and with the heavy wool sweater, wool watch cap and the CG foul weather coat, I'm still not overly warm. We ducked back into the islands by taking the lighthouse on Great Duck Island to starboard.

We sailed by a rock full of sleeping seals and we got a good look at them. As we got closer they slipped into the sea and watched us with those enormous glistening eyes emerging out of the water, until we left.

Now we are at anchor off Pond Island. I'm going to bed early tonight to fight off a cold. I've been feeding the crew members garlic pills to stop their colds, so I guess I'll take some myself.

June 21, Friday

The dawn watch was beautiful; a translucent blue and pink sky. I saw lots of seals swimming around and one mother seal was supporting a baby in front and under her almost like she was teaching it to swim. We couldn't quite figure out what she was doing and when she got close enough so we could see clearly she saw us and dove.

One small island we sailed by today must have had at least 50 seals sunning themselves. There was a lobster boat working around the island with two divers overboard. I don't know what they were looking for but someone said it might be sea urchins. Ben bought five lobsters from one of the boats working the area and we will have them for supper tonight.

As we have no wind we motored around Swan Island and went up close to the salmon farm by Burnt Coat Cove.

After lunch I went forward to relieve Chris at bow watch, but as he wanted to stay there I got permission to take a rest and fell asleep. I had woken up with THE COLD this morning, sore throat and all, so I guess I really needed the sleep. When I woke up we were under sail and driving hard. I think the cold is under control but I will continue to overdose on garlic for a while just to be sure.

We had a beautiful sail. We tacked, under sail alone, about six times and now we're back in Somes Sound for the night. We're on a mooring buoy instead of anchoring.

There is more to picking up a buoy than dropping the anchor, but it is a lot easier to get away in the morning and we won't have to have an anchor watch tonight. Tonight is the summer solstice and we have only five hours and 28 minutes of dark – Midsummer's Night.

June 22, Saturday

We got a fair start this morning but the wind was on the nose most of the way. We ran up the newly sewn jib top sail but still had to motor back to Bar Harbor. The passengers were all off boarded by noon. After lunch we stripped dirty linen and washed down the cabins. Eben showed up with the clean laundry and with everyone helping the 32 bunks were made up with clean linen in record time.

We still have time to get some things done so I volunteered to do the crew laundry and the rest of the crew will do some sanding, painting and varnishing until supper.

By 1900 I was back on the boat and Charley has watch. He wants to go out for dinner so I told him I'd cover for him until 2100. When Charley got back, Dan, Chris, George, Chris Ashcroft the prospective new owner, and I went out to a bar and stayed till closing. Chris was telling us all the fantastic plans he has for the *Harvey* when he owns it.

June 23, Sunday

This is usually a cold stove day and we have to do for ourselves for breakfast, but this morning Dave made breakfast for the crew. After breakfast I went and took a sightseeing bus to the top of Cadillac Mountain. We wound our way through Arcadia Park and the bus driver gave an excellent running dialogue about the park's history. Usually I like to go off on my own to explore an area, but there is so much here and not much time so I took the bus tour and it was a very interesting and educational trip and I'm glad that I decided to do it. We got back to Bar Harbor at noon so I bought a huge peanut butter cookie and a bowl of vanilla frozen yogurt and ate it sitting on a bench overlooking the harbor. I took a walk down to bridge road. This is a road that can be used to get to the first of the Porcupine Islands at low tide, but at high tide it is under ten feet of water. Now the tide is out so I walked about half way across and watched the gulls picking at the shells and debris that is exposed at low water. I got back to the boat and we boarded a group of Girl Scouts.

June 23, Monday

The Canadian Navy is parked next door to us this morning. There are three little ships and some very nice people. There are quite a few women on board and a couple of the women are wearing officer's caps, but I can't figure out the rank. The uniforms are black pants and a little darker than denim shirt, gold insignia on the shoulders and berets on their heads. *HMS Steele* is the name of the one parked right on the same dock we are and she seems to be the flag ship with the other two smaller ones as escorts.

Lots of fog again. Our diesel and water tanks need to be topped before we leave so we're waiting for the oil truck this morning. We are also waiting for a diver to cut the lines off the prop; one of the students from the college has volunteered for the job. When we were out at Mount Desert Rock last week we must have picked up some of those lobster lines because we can see some tangled and hanging from the shaft. The water is clear and the visibility under water is very good but it's got to be awfully cold down there.

This morning while waiting for the ship to be serviced and the fog to lift, Rich asked me to escort the Girl scouts to the COA (College of America) for a tour of the museum. We walked the one and a half miles out and I took advantage of the time to take a shower and then we walked the one and a half miles back.

Dave has bronchitis -- he went to the doctor and they charged him $162 to tell him that. Ruth has a scratchy throat and a runny nose. Rich and I are losing our voices and George has a stiff neck Interesting bug floating around – time to break out the garlic again.

By noon the fog had burned off and we had a cool brisk sail, tacking back and forth around Egg Rock. At around 4:30 Rich started the engine and we headed for Little Cranberry and Isleport again. Everyone is tired tonight- except the girl scouts - they are up on deck singing.

Almost a full moon. Venus, Mars and Saturn are in a straight line. The fog has lifted and the wind has died so it is very peaceful.

June 24, Tuesday

It is a beautiful day. We motored out to Mt. Desert Rock against a light SW wind and rode huge soft swells. We saw a couple of seals and some harbor porpoise. After circling the island a couple of times, a breeze has come up and we are sailing back into the islands. I had time to take a short nap again.

Our two cooks, Dan and Dave, have had some wild yelling matches. Dave is about six feet tall, not really fat but soft looking. He looks like he was the town fat boy when he was young and even though he has thinned down he still has that demeanor. He likes to be the center of attention and will do things to get noticed, such as climbing the rigging when everyone is on deck yelling, "Hey everyone look at me!" just like a kid. I get the impression that he is very insecure and wants approval from everybody. He also likes to make a big deal of sleeping on deck and insists that everyone give him lots of room because as cook he needs his sleep and shouldn't be disturbed. He will parade out to the foredeck with his sleeping bag and then proceed to remove suspenders and at this point I will leave so I don't really know how far he strips to go to bed. He is interested in astrology and has done quite a few of the crews' horoscopes, telling them all kinds of interesting things about their future. He is a writer and talks about the characters in his book that he is presently writing. He makes a big production of writing on his portable typewriter and makes a lot of expensive ship to shore calls to talk to his broker. He's trying to sell his business and puts all these bills on the ship's account. It should be interesting when Eben gets the bills.

Dan is about 29, good looking and trim. He loves to walk and climb rocks and will get ashore to explore any chance he gets. Neither of the cooks are real sailors but they sent in their resumes and got hired. Dave has probably done some sailing because he will take the little white hull out and sail around the boat.

Dave is still sending out resumes to everyone he can think of but Dan kind of likes this sailing and is doing more and more deck work and learning to handle lines and sail the boat. He also wants to learn celestial navigation and I believe he will. Dan is an easy going guy and very pleasant to be around and it's funny to see the two of them share the same cubby hole of a cabin. Whoever goes to bed first sleeps on his own bunk and the other one will sleep in the saloon or any place else that's open. They refuse to sleep in the same cabin.

On the way into the anchorage at McGlathary Island Rich gave me the helm for a while and I ended up staying there until we dropped the hook. We were under full sail with two head sails up and I was very pleased and surprised when he let me handle the boat as we tacked four times, and then maneuvered for the anchorage. What an experience! It takes lots of strength just to get the helm over. Quite a difference from a yacht.

When tacking, we let all the head sails fly and sheet in the mainsail. As the ship starts to head up and point into the wind, the staysail is backed and as it fills with air for the new tack it forces the bow of the boat down to the new course. I was a little nervous but it felt good to be at the helm again and although she is not as quick or responsive as a smaller boat she is very well balanced and is a dream to sail. I could get used to this very quickly.

Now we are anchored in Stonington harbor, on Deer Island, and everyone has gone ashore: Dave to get lobsters for a feed tonight and everyone else to look around. There are harbor seals and porpoises all over in here and they keep popping up to look at us. This is another lovely place with lots of little rock islands covered with pine trees and none of the islands are much bigger than a city block.

This used to be a very active harbor where the coastal schooners would pick up granite from the quarries and sail south to the markets that were building new towns and homes. The quarries are still operating and there are lobster fisherman working out of here, but things are pretty slow now.

The town is reported to be pretty "different" as there are only four families and they have lived here and intermarried for the last 200 years. They are very isolated as it's at least a two hour drive inland to the next town, and Stonington is on the ocean side of an island. Their main contact with the outside world has been by sea. Two of the crew are from Maine and they agree that the people here are a little strange. They probably are very nice but I didn't get a chance to go ashore.

Dave got $180 worth of lobsters for dinner tonight and when everyone was checked back on board we sailed out into east Penobscot Bay. What a beautiful spot. We had a great sail and there were three other schooners out enjoying the day with us. What a rush to be out here!

We sailed back into the islands by taking a bearing on the lighthouse on Great Duck Island to starboard. Coming in we passed by a rock full of sleeping seals; we got a good look at them but as we got closer they slipped into the sea and watched us until we left.

June 25, Wednesday

We are now anchored in Pulpit Harbor on North Haven Island, and the boat is swarming with girl scouts. They seem to be everywhere I look, perched on the cabin top, out on the bowsprit, down in the saloon trying to get something more to eat, and they are even climbing the rigging.

Art, our first mate, is pushing 70 but is still as agile as some of the younger crew. He's been sailing since he was 16 and has sailed all over the world. He and his wife owned the brigantine *Romance* for 23 years and they chartered in the Caribbean as a team. They sold the boat a couple years ago when it got to be too much work. He lost an eye and most of his teeth in an accident with a wrench on another ship so now he looks a little like Popeye, but he sure knows his stuff.

Before he and his wife bought their boat he was working at Mystic Seaport as a rigger and he has taught me a lot about rigging, marlinespike and other deck skills. When we're under sail, though, he gets a little over-anxious and does a lot of running around and yelling. I think that's because he's not used to a schooner. Apparently a square-rigged ship is easier to handle, and since that's what his ship was he's not as comfortable on a schooner yet. I haven't been on a square rigger, but from what I've heard they have a lot more lines to control the sails.

Art misses his "Bride" and doesn't like the cold weather of the north Atlantic. He tends to be a little irritable and forgetful at times, and will put a tool or piece of equipment down and then walk around for an hour mumbling and looking for it until either he or someone else finds the missing object. He really prefers warm weather, but after his ration of rum warms him up he's happy. Now he's doing galley duty and singing away as he shines the pots and pans.

I had watch till 2300 and all was quiet by 2230! We are tucked in Pulpit Harbor for the night and the evening was dead calm but as the tide came in we swung 180 degrees on the anchor. This is a well protected little harbor, very pretty, and the cove just SW of us belongs to the Cabot family. The sunset was spectacular and I took a picture of Pulpit Rock silhouetted against the setting sun. There is a huge osprey nest perched on top of the rock and it has been there for years, and every year the birds just keep adding to it until it looks as big as a house.

About five minutes after the sun set a full moon rose between two islands. I wasn't going to take as many pictures this trip but everything I see is postcard material.

June 26, Thursday

We left Pulpit Harbor here on North Haven Island and headed into West Penobscot Bay in a flat calm sea, and motored through Fox Island thoroughfare. What a delightful place. Then we motored over to Isle Au Haut and are now anchored in Moors Harbor where the girl scouts went ashore for a walk. The seas were calm, as we had no wind, but there were still large ocean swells. We ate lunch; the girl scouts came back all hot and sweaty from their walk. To find a better anchorage for the night we motored to a group of islands off the NE corner of Isle Au Haut called Merchant Island.

We have one midshipman on board. This is a position taken by a young person that wants to learn the art of seamanship. Alex's folks sent him to learn, but after watching him at the dinner table I think it was a cheap way to feed him. He plays football and is BIG. He prides himself on how tough he is but some of the 4H boys can outlast him on the anchor windlass and Alex is so amazed that these "skinny" little kids are tougher than him that he will talk about it all day. He is really a good kid but still very much a kid. Although he is around 15, his level of concentration is very short. This week's 4H kids all his age so he's in his glory playing games and cards with them. Not a very good way to carry his weight with the rest of the crew, and they give him a bad time about that.

I really wish he wouldn't persist in making a pest of himself by making a point of standing directly in front of me and blocking my view for at least 180 degrees when I'm on watch. He also loves to sneak up behind me and drape himself over my back and neck and call me mom.

Another crew member that came on board at St. Thomas and has been on the *Harvey* longer than some of us feels it is his duty to supervise everything the "new crew" does. He is tall and thin with curly sun-bleached hair that doesn't fall down but stands up, and a big blond beard. He hasn't been near a barber since he got on board and he's getting rather bushy. His voice is beautiful and he loves to sing sea chanteys, and will make up verses about the crew or circumstances. He is very clever and was working for the Smithsonian before joining the crew. He has a very priestly, regal manner that can be a little irritating at times, especially when he sluffs off on some of the messier jobs. This summer he was going to do volunteer work for a museum in Maine but has decided to stay on board as part of the crew.

June 27, Friday

We left our anchorage under sail this morning and had a great down wind, wing on wing running into Northeast Harbor. We stayed here for a couple of hours and I had a shower, picked up some spring water and walked around town for a while. At 4:30 we motored up Somes Sound to pick up the buoy at our favorite anchorage. We had a great birthday party for Art and after dinner, when we shot the cannon for the flag ceremony, a little ketch downwind of us returned our fire.

There are storm warnings out but I think it will pass north of us. There is some fantastic lightning but it is all NW of us and heading NE. The scouts got the whole crew mugs and presented them at a ceremony tonight. I got one with the Gloucester fisherman on it and it's really nice, besides being just like the Captain's. How about that! Both cooks had lobsters on theirs and Art's had tall ships all over it. Art sat up on deck afterwards and told stories about some of his sailing days. I wish I'd had the tape recorder on to catch some of it. The girl scouts are still singing on deck; I'm going to bed.

June 28, Saturday

The storm went NW of us and all we got was a little rain and some wind. This morning the wind was blowing about 35 knots right down the sound and we would have had a real sleigh ride down wind except the foresheet got loose as we were raising the sail and slammed across the deck. All the girl scouts were helping raise the sails, and Art was controlling the foresheet. He took all the turns off the cleat so as to keep the gaff inside the lazy jacks when a gust of wind ripped it out of his hands. Everyone got a little nervous and we were lucky no one got hurt.

A pair of tennis shoes almost got caught in the block as a crew member tried to pull it back in and one of the girls fell down trying to get out of the way and got tangled in the sheets. Luckily there was enough time to throw the sheets clear before the boom swung back across. All the kids were sent below to clear the decks and we started sailing downwind.

I was on the bow as lookout when the foresail started blowing loose and climbing up the forestay. It had been undone in preparation for raising and hadn't been retied. Ruth and I wrestled it down and secured it as well as possible. Meanwhile back on the foresail Charlie almost got knocked overboard as the foresail did an accidental jibe. At this point Rich turned the boat into the wind so we could lower and secure all sails and we motored back to Bar Harbor. Talk about a Chinese fire drill! The wind was too much right on the stern to make it safe for downwind sailing, and there isn't enough room in here to tack downwind.

We off boarded the girl scouts with lots of tears and hugs from the girls and the leaders. Nobody wanted to leave the boat after being on for a couple of days - everyone wanted to sign on as crew.

After all the passengers were ashore we proceeded to clean cabins and make up bunks for the next week's charter. Eben showed up in the middle of lunch and we motored over to the COA buoy where we will be moored for the night.

Charlie has tender duty tonight and as he wants to take a shower and call Jeanne I've volunteered to cover for him until he's done.

George has the watch tomorrow but wants to go to church so I've again volunteered to stand watch until noon. I've got to stop doing this! When he gets back I will go to town to wash some clothes, make phone calls, and drop off some film.

Chris, one of the summer crew, is 23 and going to college this fall. He's from the Boston area and has the most expensive clothes of anyone on board. His folks dropped him off at Gloucester and checked out the boat before leaving him. He is a miniature hunk and the 4H girls called him "Gorgeous." He is only five feet four and a half inches tall but built like a wrestler, very agile and strong, and always helpful, polite, and cheerful. He reminds me of the lead man in a Walt Disney movie about a shipwreck or some other adventure. When he first came on board, Art started working with him and dropped me like a hot potato - Art claims that he never would have any longhaired boys or women on his crew, and Chris is a lot stronger and more agile than I am.

Charlie is a joy. He will be 23 on the third of July and has a maturity way beyond his years. He's been working the ship since the Virgin Islands and also went to the Wooden Boat School so he is the ship's carpenter and the lead in most of the deck work. He is very good at it and all the girls idolize him. He's up and down the rigging like a monkey and always the furthest out on the bowsprit for doing the "harbor furl" - this is where the whole jib or staysail is pleated into itself and then flipped over so it looks like one long tube. It is a pretty good trick and takes about five crew members to really do it right. Charlie is always cheerful and has a line of jargon to explain anything; his vocabulary is straight out of a BIG word dictionary and almost makes sense but is absolute jumble. It's hilarious. Alex has picked up on it and he's not bad either. Pure silly fun.

The Bay of Fundy

July 13, Saturday

After everyone was off boarded I went ashore to try and find Barbara and Jim *(Barbara is Toots' sister and my mom. This trip was an unforgettable experience for Mom and Dad – Editor.)*. They were due at the boat today for a trip with us and I don't think the directions I gave them were too good. I decided to walk along the highway and let them spot me as they came into town. That's exactly what happened; they saw me as they flew by and turned around to pick me up. I was right - they had no idea of how to find the boat. They had made it this far from Minnesota by plane to Boston and then a rental car to Bar Harbor, they just weren't sure of the last few miles.

We went to Fisherman's Wharf for dinner as Jim wanted a fresh Maine lobster. He picked it right out of the tank and they boiled it for him while Barbara and I had a crab roll. We wandered around town for a little while and went into a music store where they had a concertina I had been looking at. Barbara helped pick one out that would be fairly easy to learn on and Jim insisted on buying it for me. Now we have a concertina on the boat to accompany the sea chantey singers - all I need to do is learn how to play it.

I hope Barb and Jim are happy with their cabin. They are in "Margaret," which is the most forward guest cabin, and the largest one on the boat. They have four bunks but two of them are being used for extra food storage as we are going out for two weeks this trip. We aren't a luxury liner but it is dry and private. Happy Birthday, Theresa.

July 14, Sunday

Rain! We went to town early and I got dropped off at the laundromat to get my clothes washed while Barb and Jim went to church. We went out for breakfast and then took the rental car back to the Hertz place at the airport. We got a ride back to the College from a young man using his family car as a taxi.

We have a great bunch of people on board and it looks like it will be a good trip. They are all teachers that are taking this trip for college credits.

Now the rain has stopped and the stars are starting to peek out through the clouds. Earlier this evening we saw a minke whale right here in the harbor.

2200

Everyone had just settled down and it was getting quiet when the big ferry from Nova Scotia came around the island on its way to dock. It is huge and all lit up. I called down the forward hatch to Barbara so she could come up and see the "Bluenose Ferry" coming in. She came up looking for a fairy with a blue nose.

Tomorrow early we will motor over to the city dock to take on water and diesel. Then we leave for the Bay of Fundy!

July 15, Monday

The sun is out and it's a beautiful day. We dropped the mooring at 0700 and motored over to Bar Harbor. The only spot that is open is alongside the big stone pier against the pilings. This is a very rough and dirty dock so we got out a lot of traveling fenders and carefully tied off to the pilings.

Soon the pier was lined with people looking down at us, watching our every move. The tide was out and as a ground swell would lift and drop us we would bounce off the bottom a little when it went back out - a weird feeling.

Dan, the cook, got off the ship and sat up on one of the pilings and pretended to be part of the tourist throng, asking silly questions and watching us. There were mussels and starfish tucked into the little cracks and holes of the stone pier, and we could see more of them on the bottom under the boat. They must have been stranded when the tide went out. I hope they can survive until the water comes back.

We finally got ready to go and Chris got in the tender to use it as a push boat. He pushed the stern away from the dock and then pushed in different places on the hull to help turn us in the very narrow channel.

We motored out for quite a while as there was no wind but we did see some seals, porpoises, and minke whales. There was a large disturbance on the water that looked like a bunch of little fish feeding. Apparently it was a school of little fish being pursued by four or five porpoises and there was a lot of splashing and thrashing - a real feeding frenzy. We also saw some sooty shearwaters and storm petrels. I really like the petrels - they look like they are walking on the water.

Around 1400 we headed east and now are under full sail. We will sail all night and I'm supposed to be taking a nap as I am on the 2000 to midnight watch. The stars are beautiful and I had a chance to take three star shots at dusk and will work them out later. We settled in for the watch.

I still am amazed with the fact that I'm out here, on this ship, looking up at the stars framed by the tall masts and peeking out through the sails and rigging.

We saw lots of running lights from fishing boats and what looked like the burn-off from an oil refinery. There were a bunch of red lights, like windows in a long, high, building, with three red quick-flash buoys in front of the whole thing. This was way off on the horizon towards the Maine shore. I'll see if I can find out what it is tomorrow when I can check the chart. Nobody on this watch is familiar with the area either. At midnight our watch was relieved and I'm going to bed.

July 16, Tuesday

We had a spectacular show this morning with whales and dolphins jumping out of the water, rolling around and playing all morning. I got off watch at noon and worked the star shots from last night. The star shots were right on but the moon was way off. I took a nap for about an hour and then went back on watch at 1800. Barb and Jim are having a ball and seeing lots of sea life. The white-sided dolphins are a real treat - they seem so happy and full of life. Almost like court jesters they come leaping and bounding in twos and threes in front of and around the massive black shiny backs and flukes of the whales.

The wind started to pick up and this made it harder to spot the whales but after dinner everyone was pretty tired anyway so they all went below early.

We are staying out here all night so as to be in a good position for the morning whale feedings. There is a Racon buoy that marks the entrance to the shipping channel going up into the Bay of Fundy, and we will hang around near it until dawn. I'm on watch with Rich and his sister Natalie until 2000 tonight and then on again at 0400 in the morning. I like the 0400 watch because the dawn is the best time of the day, I think. What a day of whale watching, I think I got a couple good shots of breaching whales and two jumping dolphins with even their tails out of the water.

July 17, Wednesday

At 0400 I woke up for the pre-dawn twilight and saw some morning navigation stars that I'm going to have to identify. It is very cold and the seas are lumpy. The course we need to be on puts the ship in the trough and it's throwing everything all over. We are taking a little water over the bows again but it is just making the decks a little wet.

Because the seas are so rough and we can't spot any whales among the whitecaps anyway, we put all sails up and turned towards Yarmouth, Nova Scotia. We had a beautiful sail into Yarmouth and are now tied up alongside an old decrepit fishing boat that isn't supposed to be going out tomorrow - I don't think it should ever go out by the looks of it. We will stay here tonight.

We all walked into town and I found a black sou'wester hat that is a genuine fishing hat, tarred and all, with a red plaid lining. Ruth got one too, and now there are about five of the crew that have them. The rest of the town is very much a tourist trap as this is where the *Bluenose* ferry docks, and the shops really cater to the tourists. I spotted a needlepoint canvas of the *Bluenose* schooner but as they wanted $50 for it I passed. After I thought about it for a while and decided to get it the store was closed when I went back; just as well as I really don't have time any more for sewing.

We found some great showers at the local Y and on the way back stopped in at the liquor store. Alcohol is very expensive here so we didn't get anything. We leave at 0500 so everyone is going to go to bed early for a good night's sleep.

July 18, Thursday

We left Yarmouth with the ebb tide at 0600. There was a thick fog and a fine mist that penetrated everything on board. As we passed through a fleet of Russian factory ships anchored outside the harbor, there were some of the Canadian trawlers rafted alongside these huge ships to unload their night's catch of fish. These factory ships do all the processing and packaging of the fish right on board and will stay anchored here until their holds are full of fish before they go back to Russia.

The sea is very confused and rough this morning and it is really tossing us around. As we head north into the Bay of Fundy we cross a "bar" in the middle of the bay. As we approach this area we can see the difference in the ocean. It looks like we're approaching a river with deep rapids in a powerful current. The seas around us are relatively calm but as we approach the ledge they get rougher and rougher. As we pass through the roughest water over the ledge we get thrown around some but it doesn't take long and we are out the other side. The tides up here are around 45 feet and as they flood and ebb over this ledge they make some very hazardous and perilous seas. Small boats have been swamped and lives lost our here.

The visibility is about a half mile and there are all kinds of little fishing vessels out here working the area. I wouldn't want to be here in anything smaller than the *Harvey* and even in a boat this size we can feel the turbulence.

The sun finally came out and we had a very nice sail but only saw some harbor porpoise and a couple of minke whales.

The scientific students are on a three-man lookout for trash and they are recording the time and coordinates of any and all junk that floats by, the main targets being balloons and styrofoam. Everyone seems to be taking a lot of naps on their time off. Chris and Ruth have complained of being seasick or something. It could be that everyone isn't accustomed to the 24-hour watch system yet.

The evening sail on our watch from 2000 to midnight was really nice. The moon is half full and the plankton left a wide luminous trail in our wake.

A fishing boat turned this way and came over to get a better look at us. This is always a little unnerving, having a boat head right at you at night, but Rich was familiar with the customs up here and wasn't concerned. Although he did keep a close eye on them until we were sure that's what they were doing.

Schooners are popular up in this country and they illuminated our sails and rigging with their spotlight. As they were under power and had to talk above the noise of their engines, we could hear them talking about the "sailboat" when they were still a long way off.

Rich, Natalie and I had the early watch and the three of us tacked the boat this morning without any difficulty. Of course the fact that there wasn't much wind made it easy even if it took a lot of time to come around. We didn't lose headway and made it around without going into irons (failing to make the tack) or using the engine.

July 19, Friday

During the 0800 to noon watch today I got the heads and soles done while watching some fantastic "bubble feeding." The whales will circle a school of small fish, blowing bubbles around them to herd them together. The water turns light green in the area when the bubbles get close to the surface.

One of the students was way up in the rigging and when they spotted this light green circle of bubbles on the surface of the ocean they would call out and point. This way we wouldn't miss any of the action.

When the little fish are all in a tight bunch, the whales will lunge up from underneath with their mouths wide open to scoop in as many fish as possible. Then when they close their mouths the water gushes out through the baleen but the fish are trapped inside to be swallowed. There was one large humpback and another smaller one working together so we figured it was a mother and calf. The seas and the air are filled with dolphins and greater shearwaters as the whales burst out of the sea with their mouths open spraying water and wounded fish. Again and again they vault into the air, with the dolphins diving and feeding around them and the air is filled with the screeching of the white, soaring, diving birds.

Rich cut the engine and we drifted through this spectacular display for a long time. The whole show was a symphony of movement and I wish it could have been put to music but it is a scene in my head that I'll never forget. What a fantastic show.

After this was over, Barbara, Natalie and I washed the decks down with buckets of salt water and then it was time for lunch and our watch was over.

The engine is back on and we're on the way to another spot where whales have been spotted. I'm going to try and take a nap before it's time for our watch again. It's very hazy and hard to spot anything unless it's right under the boat. The engine was killed and we sat silent in the water. Off to starboard we could hear some whales feeding and blowing but couldn't see a thing.

We took the long channel into Briar Island and docked at the main dock right downtown. Rich turned the boat around and backed into the dock. The current was vicious and wouldn't let the stern come over. The whole town came down to see us and everyone is very helpful and friendly. One of the scientists laughingly commented that we were the highlight of the season and they would talk for years to come about the day the schooner came to the island. "Remember the day that big schooner came down the channel, loaded with women and everyone eating fried chicken up on the deck?" Must be pretty quiet around here. We topped off the diesel and water and one of the guys from town offered to get us some ice with his pickup truck.

After we were finished at the dock we tried to pick up a mooring in the harbor but it was so encrusted with seaweed and shells that we finally gave up, went further out into the harbor and set a hook.

The six-knot rip tide running out through this narrow cut is a powerful current with huge standing waves that make a noise like a waterfall or a roaring rapids. If you fell in here at ebb tide it would probably be the last anyone would see of you.

The flowers are fabulous and the trees are all stunted and gnarled from the wind. Everything is shrouded in mist and fog and looks very mysterious and beautiful.

July 20, Saturday

We are socked in solid. Everyone kind of wandered around town all afternoon. Talked to some of the people and explored a little of the village. We will stay here tonight because of the heavy seas and fog outside.

A lot of the staff from the whale watching station were invited out to the boat for a rum punch reception and roast beef dinner and I had tender duty. Landing the tender alongside the boat is kind of fun, like bringing a boat into a floating dock against a six-knot current.

July 21, Sunday

There is still solid fog in the harbor but we will be leaving around 1000 with the high slack tide. The reports are that there is less fog out on the ocean, in the lee of Long Island.

Even at near slack tide we had a good current and as we got out into the open the fog lifted a little and we had about one and a half miles of visibility. We spotted two humpbacks logging *(so-called because they look like floating logs)* on the surface and stayed with them for a little while but as they didn't wake up we moved on. It's not very interesting watching whales sleep.

The *Venture,* the whale watching boat out of Briar Island, was out here too but we parted ways and she went north while we went west towards Grand Manan Island. We didn't see much of anything all day until around 1600 when a right whale was spotted. We went over to where he dove, and waited. He finally blew right under the starboard side of the boat and scared everyone. There was a mad rush as everyone ran to get pictures and I think I got a picture of his blow hole from behind but then he was gone. Rich is really good at thinking like a whale and being at just the right place when they come up.

It started to rain hard so I went down for a nap before it is my turn to go back on watch. Today I'm off watch at 1600 back on at 2000 to midnight. We are anchored outside the breakwater but in the harbor at Grand Manan. We will stay here tonight and I have tender duty.

It was pretty late by the time we were secure for the night but everyone wanted to go ashore so I made a couple of runs in the tender and then came back to the boat. The first pickup at 2000 was a little late as it was a pretty good trip into the floating dock and things look different in the dark. When I got there at 2015 the only ones waiting were Barbara and Molly. They said everyone else was at the bar or walking out to the lighthouse.

We no more than got out to the boat and the tender tied up when the Captain called on his radio and wanted to know why I left so early! I went back and picked him up and by the time he was on board it was time to make the 2100 run. This took two boat loads so I thought I was done for the night. After a head count we are two short! One more trip to pick up the last passengers and then I really am done for the night. I really think we should synchronize our watches.

The stars are out and the breeze feels warm and sweet off the land.

July 22, Monday

Beautiful sunny morning. The Captain volunteered to do the heads for our watch this morning so I could get to town for a while. I had an hour so I walked to the beach under the lighthouse and picked up some sea glass. On the way back I stopped in a little store and got a new cup. The handle on mine had been broken and while it was waiting for Charley to glue it I think Dave the cook threw it out.

We left the harbor under sail but the wind soon died and we are motoring again. We crossed the "bar." I don't think it's the same one we crossed before but it was pretty spectacular. It's rough even in this dead calm today with whirl pools and standing waves, but I can imagine what it would be like with wind and a running sea. A man and his son got caught in it last week some time and they both drowned.

No whales today - only one seal and some harbor porpoise.

July 23, Tuesday
At 0400 when it was still too dark to see anything we could hear whales all around us - tail slapping and doing lots of splashing and blowing.

The sun came up blood red, coloring the ominous angry clouds on the horizon. We have all the signs for a good storm brewing- even the mackerel sky!

By 0800 we had come up close to a couple of right whales - a mom and baby, so we stayed with them for quite a while. They are a little boring to watch though as all they do is swim along with their mouths open eating plankton.

It started to sprinkle and we spotted three humpbacks that gave us a spectacular show of tail whacking, rolling around and waving and just general goofing off. I'm getting soaked and chilled in this sprinkle so I guess I'd better go below and dry off before it's our watch again

Barbara woke me from a dead sleep to see a shark that is right off our bow. He was lying just below the surface with his triangular fin sticking out of the water just like in the movies. I took his picture as he was right under the bow and he turned and dove. He must have been sleeping and we woke him up. He was brownish grey with white splotches on his body back by the tail.

It's raining and getting pretty messy out now. We're under sail and moving along at around seven knots. I'm torn between staying down here where it is just damp or going up on deck where it is very wet. I'm off till 1600 so I guess I'd better stay down here and get some rest.

At 1330 I was jerked awake as a huge wave came from nowhere and slapped the bow of the boat. It made a loud thump like hitting something solid and I started to go topside to check it out. Just as I headed up to the deck, there were a group of people trying to carry Nan back aft. It was very difficult as the ship was being thrown around pretty bad and it is pouring rain. It seems that there were a lot of people up on the forward part of the boat enjoying the sail and a rogue wave took them off balance.

Barb and Jim got knocked over with the rest of them and Nan somehow got her finger stuck on the forecastle hatch door and ripped the end of her left index finger completely off. She almost slammed her head against the starboard anchor as the boat rolled but a couple of people saw her sliding and grabbed her.

As she was complaining about her leg they helped her crawl aft, not even aware at this time that the worst injury was her finger. As I was coming up the companionway, she was coming down so I helped settle her in the saloon. We splinted her left leg using towels and the slats from the radar box and at this time she was still more concerned about her leg than her finger.

We did all the classic first aid with warm blankets and elevated feet as she was pretty shocky. One of the teachers had just finished her EMT training and this was her first real victim but between my expired EMT and her brand new one I think we did a pretty good job. Nan responded very well and the color started to come back into her face. Thank goodness Ruth, who is a nurse, showed up because when we took Nan's gloves off to warm her up and found the missing finger Ruth took care of wrapping it, icing it down and getting it ready to send with Nan to the Hospital. Ruth also handled all the radio conversations with the doctors about medications and such. When we found the missing finger joint and realized what had happened, Rich got on the radio and we had a lot of radio traffic between us, the CG- COA and Eben while we made a bee line for Bar Harbor.

I was relieved of my regular watch because I was one of the few that could stay below without getting seasick or nervous about taking care of Nan. The other passenger who is an EMT was great for the initial splinting and such but got seasick very quickly staying down here in the saloon. Nan seems to be content and relaxed holding my hand.

We had a very rough and noisy ride back for at least seven hours and the storm was really roaring. Everything in the saloon was flying around and a cooler full of red cool aid tipped over. When I heard the sloshing and looked down to see this red liquid pooled at my feet my first thought was blood.

We got to Bar Harbor in the thickest fog I've seen so far, the kind of fog that the *Flying Dutchman* (a legendary ghost ship) sails in. Now that the seas have flattened out in the lee of the land, I'm back on bow watch. I kept seeing imaginary square riggers in the swirling fog, but as I looked right at them they'd disappear.

Rich made a beautiful eggshell landing at a dock we couldn't see until it was so close we could just hand the lines over to the people anxiously waiting for us on the dock. They said they couldn't see the hull until the bowsprit was over the dock. We were met by the ambulance drivers with a gurney for Nan, the Customs and Immigration officers, Eben, and Ted from the COA.
After Nan was shipped off to a Boston Hospital where her daughter is a doctor, the crew that was off duty went ashore for a well-deserved break.

July 24, Wednesday
Today I have the day off. We are still tied to the dock at Bar Harbor and, as Barb and Jim need to get another rental car, the Harbor master has offered to give Jim a ride into the airport to pick one up. Barbara and I unloaded their luggage and took it ashore to wait for Jim, as the boat has to move off the city dock before noon and it is easier to take the luggage off here at the city dock in downtown Bar Harbor than at the mooring over at the college, where we would have to load everything into the tender and carry all the luggage up the steep hill after unloading it on the dock. There is also that steep set of stairs if the tide is out.

We sat on the side of a hill in the shade as the boat moved away from the dock and back over to the COA mooring buoy. It was a strange feeling watching the *Harvey* pull away from the dock and leave without me. We watched her round the Porcupine Islands and disappear.

While we were waiting I went into a little store and found the exact replica of the cup that had been broken, so I bought it to take back to the boat. Jim finally showed up and we rode back to the college in their rental car to make use of the showers and wash some clothes. After we had some lunch and walked through the gardens at the college once more, Barb and Jim had to leave. I hate goodbyes and I really felt bad, and lonesome, when they left but we had a great ten days even if it went by too fast.

I went out to the ship and tried to take a nap but didn't have any luck so I came out into the saloon to join Rich, Dave, and Art in a little rum and some conversation. Dan fixed a great scallop dinner and then Rich, Ruth and I walked into town and had a drink at the "Greenhouse." We returned to the boat early and Eben showed up to ask everyone a lot of questions about the accident.

Celestial Navigation

July 31, Wednesday

Clear, cold, and calm. We headed out into big swells and the promise of rain. We ran down east for a while and then got a call about a humpback spotted in Frenchman's Bay right by the Porcupine Islands, almost in sight of Bar Harbor.

When we first saw him he was breaching clean out of the water and kept doing it over and over. We are in hot pursuit and as we get closer it's clear that this is just a small young humpback and he is going crazy. He breached right next to the boat five times in a row and then proceeded to do a lot of tail slapping and rolling around. He would roll over on his back and throw his long white flippers around almost as if he were waving at us. We were finally getting a chance to show this group a whale up close and give them a chance to watch it when the Arcadia whale watching boat came boiling up behind us and proceeded to harass (get way too close and even running over the place he had just gone down) the whale. They pushed in between us and blocked our view. Finally the whale had enough and left. He just dove and didn't come up.

The whale watching boat could maneuver much better with its greater speed but it was very poor manners on his part to move in like that. All the students wanted to light the cannon and blow him out of the water. The whale had disappeared so we headed NE again and the whale watching boat went up into the bay looking for him.

I put on my lucky Briar Island sweatshirt with the picture of the humpbacks on it and guaranteed everyone we would see some more whales. We spotted the whale again and had a couple of hours to watch and track him. This was the most activity this group has had and they thanked me profusely, with tongue in cheek, for bringing the whale to us. It works every time!

The fog moved in and we headed into Winter Harbor which is just "Down East" from Bar Harbor. It's a short distance by water but a long way around by land and it's pretty isolated. Again I didn't go ashore as Ruth was running the tender for the first time on her own, in a strange place, after dark and in the fog, so I stayed on board for moral support with the radio and a flashlight to signal our position.

Chris had the watch but he wanted to go ashore to make a phone call so, as I really didn't care anyway, I took the watch for him and when he got back we played some chess. He took the first three games but I finally got him on the fourth. Every one gave a good report of the town and had a good time dancing at a local bar.

This is a real pretty little harbor and doesn't look like a tourist town at all. Maybe next time I'll go ashore here.

August 1, Thursday

We picked up the humpback right outside the harbor entrance almost like he was waiting for us. We are under sail heading out to Mt Desert Rock. It's a beautiful day as the sun has finally come out and we have a nice breeze. I got to go down in the chain locker again this morning and after I finished the heads, soles, and ladders I went on the bow to do lookout and watch for whales.

Now we are way out past Mt. Desert rock and heading southwest. Kevin and Peter, the instructors for this trip, want to spend the night our here again and try once more for a morning show of whales. The blower motor on the stove is dead again after Charlie replaced it with the last rebuilt motor on board, so we will have to eat cold food and no coffee. Rich is worried about the weather forecast but Peter is insisting we stay out anyway.

There isn't much activity this afternoon, a school of dolphins went by in the distance, jumping and feeding, but it's a great sailing day. I tried to take a nap but every time I'd doze off they would tack. I went on deck to help but as I have the midnight to 0400 watch tonight I'll have to go below and get some sleep. Though it's almost balmy now I have my wool socks, sweater and hat ready to go as I'm sure it will be cold in the early morning hours. It's a beautiful warm evening and I hate to leave the deck. We took the main down and are sailing under fore and staysail only so the boat can be handled with a small crew.

August 2, Friday

The weather deteriorated and the 2000 - midnight watch hove to. It was very rough below with things flying all over again. There was a Pan-Pan on the radio for a boat that is overdue and another Pan-Pan for some red flares spotted by Egg Rock. Not much sleep for anyone and at midnight our watch was on.

Rich and Kevin decided to sail instead of sitting here getting beat up. As we started to sail the motion of the boat eased a lot but without a main sail we had a pretty heavy lee helm and the schooner was a bear to hold on course. I stuck my foot in my mouth because as I came on deck I asked whose idea it was to stay out here anyway - and of course it was Peter's and he was right there!

After my hour at the helm I turned it over to someone else and started making the rounds for the log entry. He over-steered and we got in irons Charlie turned the engine on and we got back on course but the engine noise brought Rich up on deck. He did some plotting and changed course to 295 and we headed for Duck Island. The huge seas we were in were right on the beam so it made for a very interesting ride.

The squalls around us were visible on the radar screen even if we couldn't see them in the pitch dark. We barely outran two spectacular electrical storms by pushing the speed up to seven knots. We watched it creep up on us on the radar and then we could see it pass behind us on the screen and see the bolts of lightning hit the water in our wake. Very interesting!

At 0300 I asked Charlie to relieve me at the helm as my arms were getting tired and I was having difficulty holding a straight course. We had just had a close encounter with a very fast boat that had a weird light configuration: White over red like a pilot boat but no running lights. As he came right at us, on our port side, I could see the bow wake and swung to starboard to get out of his way. He passed in front of us and we resumed course. Rich and Charlie were watching him through the glasses and they didn't know what he was. My arms were pretty shaky but we didn't bump. Charlie wanted to know why I changed course without asking him. I suppose I should have waited for an order but that boat was getting awfully close and he didn't act like he even saw us at all. My reflex was to get out of his way.

Woke up to a beautiful, calm, sunny day moored in Somes Sound. Rich is in good humor and is joking around and climbing the rigging. I think this is his way of relieving tension after a particularly hairy trip. He had the 0400 - 0800 watch that brought us into Somes but he had been on call all night and didn't get much sleep.

We will go to Bar Harbor to drop off this charter and pick up the extra crew for the two-day trip to Boston. It will be an off shore run with Eben and Shirley, and their friends Doug and Mary, on board for the trip. We'll have one hour to shower and get back on board before we leave.

Eben, Doug and I have the 2000 - midnight watch and we are actually doing DR (dead reckoning) plotting on the chart. The wind is calm so we are motoring and the course is laid out behind Duck Island and then past Long Island. At this time we will set a course for Martinicius Rock. This is going to be a fun trip. The moon came up like a fire on the horizon and it's a beautiful evening.

August 3, Saturday

We did sun shots this morning! Worked out a running fix with the LAN and it was right on! When Eben saw it he told Rich to "eat your heart out" as he never got that close in his wildest dreams.

A little later as Rich was hosing down the deck with the fire hose he "accidently" ricocheted a powerful stream of salt water all over my sextant and me. I hope it was an accident.

We're cleaning cabins and just finished the mid-ship compartment. I had watch from 1800 to 2000 and it was a very quiet day. Now I'm going to try to take a nap as we will be running all night. ETA Boston is 0800 tomorrow morning. Rich is leaving for two weeks and doesn't seem to be very happy about that. The Boston Aquarium group that has chartered us has requested another Captain, the one that they had last year, so he will replace Rich for the two weeks.

Rich seems very distracted but he's been up and down since I've known him so I guess I'll just ignore his moods. He's cleaning out his cabin for the new Captain and just returned my three cruising books for the Maine coast. I got my chart for the Gulf of Maine back also. We are in a transition period and a lot of the crew will be leaving or taking vacations. Both Ruth and Rich are sleeping in clean cabins that were just made up.

August 4, Sunday

We arrived in Boston at 0845 after an uneventful night. The air is different: Hot and rather pungent after Maine. Eben brought the boat to the dock after doing a 180 in a very small space. It's pouring and we have just finished the bunks and most of the cleanup. Next, a shower and laundry.

Rob drove all the way down to see me and brought Becky and David. They stayed for a couple of hours as we toured the ship and then they drove back to Raymond. I'm tired and a little lonesome so I guess I'll hit the sack and get some sleep. It's been a long three days and it takes a while to get used to a 24-hour watch schedule. Two days isn't enough to settle in. Tomorrow we start a new charter with a new Captain in a new area.

August 5, Monday

We left pier seven in Boston at 1000. Every bunk in the boat is full. Even the crew quarters in the forecastle have all four bunks occupied. Our midshipman stayed in Boston to attend the computer show. The only bunk open for him was down in the forecastle and he claims he can't climb the ladder either in or out. It is pretty steep and drops down at least seven feet to the deck through a rather small hatch.

Captain Will Gates is our Captain for the next two weeks. He did this trip for the Boston Aquarium last year and they requested him again. This charter is through the Boston Aquarium and we have some of their staff, plus some whale experts from California with us. I like having naturalists aboard as they can identify a lot of sea life for me and they love to answer questions.

As there was no wind we motored out to Stellwaggon Banks through some huge swells. The going was pretty slow and because of the rough swells we didn't spot any whales so we headed back towards land and are now tied at our old spot in Gloucester. Feels like coming home.

August 6, Tuesday

We got a very early start this morning to get out to Stellwaggon Banks and hopefully find some whales. There were big, huge swells again and very little wind. The whales were feeding and although we did see some fins and tails as they dove to feed, there wasn't anything spectacular. Maybe everything else looks tame after all the magnificent activity we saw in the Bay of Fundy. Everyone I've talked to on this trip seems to be happy with the whales they're seeing now but they have never even heard of bubble feeding much less seen it so I guess I am very lucky.

Tonight we anchored at Rockport outside the breakwater, so there will be an anchor watch all night. Captain Will first took the Harvey inside the harbor to off-board the guests. We got permission to raft against another schooner tied at the dock so the passengers could climb across her decks to get ashore. There isn't enough water in here to float the Harvey at low tide so we did a 180 in very close quarters, with the help of the harbor master in his Boston Whaler, and came out here to anchor.

Captain Will Gates works for the state of Maryland as the full time Captain of the museum ship *The Dove*. He is very patient and is an excellent teacher, showing us, with great detail, how he wants lines coiled and sheets handled while he's aboard. This kind of training is important for a new Captain as it makes for a better and smoother working crew. We all know exactly what is expected of each of us in any maneuver. Will does a great job handling this boat. He is very traditional, does things by the book, and I feel comfortable with him; he seems to have gone through the same basic seamanship training that I did.

August 7, Wednesday

We left before breakfast and sailing this ship is interesting with a shorthanded crew. Ruth went into the chain locker and I took over both Art's and Alex's jobs. I stood up on the bow and signaled the helmsman where the anchor was and when it broke loose with arm signals. Then I got to jump down to ring the bell. One bell for the anchor chain being straight up and down, two bells when the anchor breaks loose and we are underway, and three bells when the ring is out of the water. Just as soon as we have broken loose from the bottom, the anchor ball has to be lowered and the crew with the anchor burton stands by to complete the job. It gets pretty busy on the bow while all this is going on. With most of the more seasoned crew on leave, we "new" crew are getting to do more of the actual handling of the ship and it is very satisfying.

Mare's tails and mackerel skies this morning, but now the sky has cleared off and it's hot and still. Conroy, one of the passengers, has been learning celestial and is getting pretty good. He took some shots today and is doing the sight reductions with just a little prompting. I love teaching celestial and he is a quick student and has been taking reams of notes.

Lots of whales today. One was breaching right next to the boat and everyone was happy and excited to be so close and getting such good pictures.

Whenever a whale starts putting on a good show, breaching and tail slapping, every whale watching boat in the area comes screaming over to give their paying customers their money's worth. I can't blame them for wanting to satisfy their customers but it's really not fair to cut us off in our slower moving boat.

There are a lot of whale watching boats in this area and sometimes it's more fun watching them than the whales. They like to maneuver so when they get a picture of a whale, the schooner is in the background. One day three of us sitting on the lister box did the "see no evil, hear no evil, speak no evil" monkeys as a tourist boat came close to take pictures. I wonder if they came out.

It is very hot and still today. Halfway between Stellwaggon Bank and the mainland, out where the shore is just a smudge on the horizon, Will cut the engine and had a swim call! When the ship had come to a complete stop we had a half hour to go swimming. I didn't dive in like some of the more adventuresome crew but I did back down and swim long enough to wash my hair and find out that the North Atlantic is very cold! I actually went swimming in the Atlantic, 20 miles from shore, with huge whales and other denizens of the deep lurking below.

Now we are moored to a town buoy in Marblehead for the night and we seem to be quite an attraction. There must not be very many schooners that spend the night here and she looks huge among all the beautiful classic yachts that are moored nearby.

As we were coming into the anchorage, there were a lot of boats out cruising around and it seemed like everyone made a point of coming closer to get a good look. The Wednesday night regatta fleet sailed right by us on the way back to their moorings after their race and it was fun watching all those beautiful yachts up close.

We made a star identification tonight and found out it was a planet! Vega. There doesn't seem to be any luminous algae in this harbor. I wonder why?

August 8, Thursday

Even though we were on a mooring buoy we had anchor watch last night. There are a lot of boats in a very small area and there is always the danger of swinging over someone when the tide turns.

At least it's not an active watch. The first watch makes the rounds of the ship, checks the mooring, makes the log entry and sets an alarm clock for the next watch. When the alarm goes off the crew that has that watch gets up, makes the rounds, sets the clock for the next watch, puts it near them and goes back to sleep. This system works very well and no one loses too much rest

This morning we are still in Marblehead as a lot of the guests want to explore the town, and the rest of them are sick with some kind of flu bug. Lots of traffic in the heads last night. Even some of the crew are sick; in fact the only crew that are still up and around are Dan the cook, Ruth, Chris, and myself. Charlie is really feeling bad but at least he is up on deck in case we really need him .He's sleeping and looks bad. Captain Will is up but looking a little green around the gills. Mike and Barrett, the naturalists from the aquarium, are down for the count also.

We are hoping it's only the 24-hour bug. At least it can't be the food because we all ate the same thing and we aren't all sick.

August 9, Friday

By dinner time last night everyone was starting to feel a little better although still a little weak.

After spending the night in Gloucester we left bright and early to go back to Stellwaggon Bank. The whales were spectacular this morning with lots of acrobatics. This is a good finale for the week, and we need one what with the lack of wind and whales and the flu that put everyone under the weather. Having the whales show up this morning was good for everyone's morale.

The wind has picked up and we are now under full sail and heading back to Boston. This is the first decent wind we've had all week and even though it's overcast and starting to rain it's nice to have the engine off and the boat alive. It's funny but I've noticed the whales always seem to get more active before a rain storm.

Charlie is starting to feel better and I'm sure glad because my arms are starting to feel like putty from running this ship with a skeleton crew. Ruth got sick this morning.

We had a glorious sail into Boston and had dinner on deck as we sailed in. There was roast beef, mashed potatoes and gravy with apple pie for desert. I'm happy to see everyone's appetite returning.

Tonight we are rafted to the *Adventure* at the World Trade Center for the big celebration here tomorrow to promote "Sail Boston '92," and with all the schooners coming here to help celebrate there isn't enough dock to go around.

August 10, Saturday

Pouring rain! We set the big awning up under the foresail and put the tarp over the saloon skylight to try and keep a little dry. The passengers started to leave but again no one wanted to go. There is something about this ship that makes people feel very much at home and they want to sign on. Even with the lack of wind and not many whales, a week of flu and now the rain, everyone had a good time and we got the biggest tip ever!

 The laundry needs to be done again so everyone helped load it into Eben's van and he drove me over to the south side of Boston and dropped me off at a laundromat with instructions to get a cab when I was done. There were seven loads again and I had high hopes of all the cabins clean and neat by the time I got back but no luck.

The boat was swarming with people for the "Sail Boston" open house so I ducked into the midsection and got those bunks made up anyway.

The *Adventure, Black Pearl, Spirit of Massachusetts*, three older excellent twelve-meters, and a group of smaller classic wooden schooners and ketches are tied along the pier with us. The open house and promotion for "Sail Boston 92" is in full swing with a reception for all the crews up on the pier. Lots of food and an open bar. The sun broke out and it ended up as a beautiful evening.

August 11, Sunday

A bunch of us went to the Boston Aquarium this morning. Wow, what a place. I wish we had more time to wander. The sharks were fascinating but I'm not too sure about going swimming out there anymore.

August 12. Monday

We left the dock in Boston at 0900 and as soon as we were clear of the slip the command to raise sails was given. I glanced back as we were raising our staysail and noticed the *Adventure* out in the middle of the harbor getting ready to raise her sails also. We started down channel towards the ocean with the *Adventure* not far behind - looks like we might have a race going.

We tacked back and forth across the channel against a stiff breeze and a flood tide, with the *Adventure* close on our heels. Her longer waterline and deeper keel give her the advantage in speed. She can also point higher on the wind without as much leeway slip.

She kept gaining on us with each tack and must have gained at least a boat length. We were tacking across the main channel when the CG cutter *Escanaba* (#907) came down the channel heading out to sea. We will have to cross her bow or drop behind her which would effectively give the *Adventure* the race. We had the right of way, but she is the CG and a lot bigger!

But before our Captain made a decision, *Escanaba* stopped, signaled three short blasts, (which means her engines are in stern propulsion) and held station as we sailed in front of her. Excellent!

Later we came into a crossing situation with the *Adventure* in which we had the right of way, being on a starboard tack. She would have to give way and pass behind us. But, to make things interesting, coming down the channel was another CG cutter, the *Spencer* (#905) and we had the right of way over her also. But our Captain decided it was not worth the effort so he turned the engine on and got out of the way of both of them.

The *Adventure* passed us and we sailed in her wake all the way to Gloucester where we are now tied up at the gas dock. I did get some great pictures of her and as this is her "maiden voyage" since she's been rebuilt I'll get a set of prints for the crew.

We had a beautiful sail and there are three passengers this trip that want to learn celestial. I got them started and every time I do this I get more organized in my thinking.

August 13, Tuesday

We left at 0630 before anyone but the crew was up and headed for Stellwaggon Bank. One whale started breaching just when we got out there and we had quite a show. We have a team of photographers aboard from Germany's Geo magazine and they are snapping pictures all the time. I'm glad the one whale was getting so close. The pictures I've seen that they took are so beautiful and detailed that you can see the barnacles and drops of water on the whale's flukes.

It was very hot and the plan was to stop for a swim on the way back to port. We left the banks at 1400 and even though I was sure a shark would bite me I was going to go swimming again. Instead I fell asleep and woke up just outside Thatcher Island.

Herman, the photographer from Germany, has a swollen jaw and is in a lot of pain. We are going to get him to town before the dentist's office closes. I have tender duty tonight and I get to ride the tender down while we are still underway - this will save time and we can go directly to the dock and not wait till the anchor is down.

The tender is hung by a series of blocks and tackles at the stern of the boat. I climbed into the tender, put the plugs in, checked the gas and motor, and gave the signal that I was ready to go. The crew lowered me down to the water stern first and I released the stern tackle. At this point I'm being towed behind the schooner by the bow tackle. The motor starts right up and I put it in slow forward gear which allows me to go forward and release the bow hook. While this is going on the rest of the crew have put the boarding ladder over and I have the fun of pulling up alongside and grabbing it while we are both underway. A crew member handed me the painter as I came alongside so Herman, Doris, and Mike could come aboard and we headed for town.

It's a pretty good run into Rockport from out here and by the time I had dropped them off at the Rockport dock and got back to the boat the hook was down and it was time for dinner.

I'm on tender duty until 2400 and it is a beautiful evening. Clear skies, a light breeze, and the water is full of florescent algae again. A flashlight shone into the water seems to attract them and after a few minutes you can turn the light off and there is a pool of little bright lights -- like stars in the water.

August 14, Wednesday
Up and out again at 0630. I got the chain locker this morning.

We had a great show this morning out on the banks and the humpbacks were so close we could almost touch them. I got whales' breath all over me! We even had some "spy hopping" where the whales come partially out of the water in a more controlled way to look at us - or so it seems.

I'm sure tired. We have some more "seasicks" on board but not as many as last week. I've started carrying plastic bags in my pocket just in case someone feels sick on deck. I get a little nervous when anyone starts heaving over the side - I'm afraid they'll fall in.

We hove to for a swim break and today I went in. The North Atlantic is very cold and salty, but refreshing. All the sails are up but we backed the staysail and put the helm hard over so we aren't going anywhere very fast, just sliding down wind a little. The swim ladder was put over the side and we deployed a life ring on a line. Just about every one dove in but sissy me backed down the ladder and slid in. The salt water felt good but I didn't stay long as I'm still sure there is a shark under the boat eyeing my foot and waiting for the right moment to take a bite.

The swim woke me up a little but I'm still exhausted. I didn't get the flu like the rest of the crew and passengers but I'm stiff all over and have a cold sore so I must be pretty run down. I sure hope I don't get the "bug."

The *Eagle* is under full sail but so far away the camera wouldn't be able to take a picture of her. Now is when I wish I had a big power boat to be able to fly out there and take some pictures.

We are at the mooring buoy at Marblehead again tonight and after making a trip into town with Ruth to get ice, I've decided to stay aboard and catch up on some sleep rather than making the town with the crew. As we came in tonight the racing fleet was just leaving and most of them came close by to wave and smile at us. Very friendly people and it was a real treat to see all these beautiful racing yachts parade by our boat with crews dressed in the latest racing clothes. Quite a fashion show! Another beautiful clear evening but the flies are biting so I suppose it will rain tomorrow.

August 15, Thursday

Another early start, with the wind just perfect for sailing off the mooring. We raised the fore and the staysail, slipped the mooring and glided out of the harbor. A little minke whale came right over to the boat and swam across our bow, almost as if it was looking us over.

There was a little harbor seal way out here out of sight of land and I wonder if it is lost. It circled the boat a couple of times and kept lifting the upper part of its body out of the water looking at us. It almost looked like it wanted to come on board. He sure looked confused and lost and not very big at all. I hope he makes it and that shark doesn't get him.

We have overcast skies and after lunch it started pouring. After the first few whales we saw when we got out this morning, we didn't see anything all day and now we are tied next to the *Adventure* in Gloucester.

It's hot and muggy and a long way from the showers. Dan and I walked to Rocky Neck, back where we were in drydock this spring, and stopped in the piano bar for a cold beer. We had just gotten there when Herman and Doris walked in. They had come back to the boat after going to town and couldn't find me. Charlie knew where we had gone so they bribed him to run them over in the tender. Herman's tooth seems to be better and we had a couple of COLD beers and hitched a ride back to the boat with two ladies that were sitting at the next table. They were from Canada and had struck up a conversation with us so when we were ready to leave they offered to give us a ride. The car wasn't very big but we managed to squeeze in and have a cozy trip back to the boat. It was quite a way back and to ***not*** have to walk home was appreciated.

August 16, Friday

We had a beautiful sail out to the banks this morning but it seems that when the weather is good for sailing it's lousy for spotting whales. We did see some but not as close as the other day. Herman wasn't very happy as he had come here specially to get pictures of whales. He has gotten some spectacular shots I think, but we didn't get close enough today.

Instead of going directly into Boston tonight, we anchored at an island just outside the harbor, and a little west along the coast. I never realized there were so many pretty little islands along the coast here outside Boston.

One of the passengers had brought his video camera and the day the whales were so close he took lots of pictures. Tonight the TV was set up on deck and we got to watch the whole thing again. The pictures were great and he got some fantastic footage.

August 17, Saturday

We motored into pier 7 this morning and off boarded the guests. I hated to see Herman and Doris leave as I had really enjoyed their company, but they had another trip planned in the Bay of Fundy to get more whale pictures. Hopefully some bubble feeding.

We had just started cleaning cabins when my son Rob showed up. I must have looked pretty shot last weekend when he stopped by because he insisted I come back home with him and spend the weekend. It had been a rough week, what with some of the crew taking time off and the rest of them getting sick, but I didn't think I was that tired. Anyway, even if there was a lot to do before we boarded the next charter, I was told to get out of there and enjoy the weekend. It didn't take long to throw a few things in a duffle and we were on the way to New Hampshire.

When we arrived there was hardly time to turn around before all the kids were in the car and we were on our way to go swimming in a warm, freshwater lake. Afterwards we had a barbecue in the back yard. Rob keeps telling me I can stay with him and I don't have to go back to the boat. He seems to think it's too much work for me. But I love it and am not ready to stay ashore yet.

August19, Monday

 There wasn't anything unusual about the sky this morning as we drove back to Boston, but when we got to the boat and Rob dropped me off, everyone was busy lashing gear down. There is a possibility that a hurricane may come this way!

I got to go out on the boom and remove the jib topsail. That's a nice vantage point way up in the air looking back at the full length of the boat and I sat up there, straddling the jib boom, taking the hanks off the jib and feeding the sail back down to the deck. When that was done and the sail was rolled and securely lashed to the deck, I helped the rest of the crew and now we are all lashed down and have removed everything from the decks that might blow away or catch too much wind. Rob and another coastie stopped by in full regulation gear to check on our condition and then he left for home. I feel we're safer here on the boat than he will be driving on the highway.

Most of the crew chose to stay aboard but Eben off-boarded the passengers and put them up in a hotel in town. We started the wait. There wasn't a lot to do except check for chafing, listen to the wind grow, and walk out to the end of the dock now and then to see what the ocean looks like now. The wind got hard to walk against as the evening came closer and the walk out to the end of the dock where it was more open to the sea became more of a challenge. The harbor looks pretty mean - not big seas, because there isn't enough room to let them build, but very impressive waves with the spume blowing straight off the top of the whitecaps. Back inside the protection of the tall city buildings the *Harvey* was pretty well sheltered from the wind. The real danger here was flying debris. The tin roof from a shed flew across the docks and landed against a pile of big fuel drums just in front of us. The Tobin Bridge is closed to traffic and there is lots of wind and rain. Looks like we're going to have a hurricane!

At 1800 I got through to Rob and he had made it home okay but there are trees down all over and they had ten inches of rain already. I went below into my cocoon of a cabin and took a nap for a couple of hours and the storm never got bad enough to wake me up. When the wind started to lessen and shift around, the squeaking from the fenders rubbing against the dock as the wind crushed us hard against them stopped, and I think the lack of noise is what woke me up.

The storm was mild here and I think that Hurricane Bob fizzled when the eye passed over Cape Cod. The winds here never got over 65 knots and although we did get some pretty heavy rain, it was no worse than a good Minnesota storm.

When the wind started to diminish it shifted and backed to the west, and then SW, and by 2100 the moon peeked out and the sky started to clear off.

August 20, Tuesday
Rich is our Captain again as Will has gone back to his ship, but Rich's family's home is on the Cape and they got hit bad so Rich is going down to help them, and Eben will take the *Harvey* out today.

The *Harvey* is Eben's boat and he has been driving it since it was first launched. He handles this 100- ton schooner like it was a little sports car and is very relaxed.

The after effects of the hurricane are still with us; we just had a torrential downpour and we're supposed to have rain showers off and on all day. It's kind of an eerie feeling heading out into the ocean where only yesterday there was a hurricane raging. Everything still looks a little ominous with dark racing clouds and wind. Tomorrow is promised to be nicer.

When we got to Stellwaggon it was pouring again but we saw a lot of whales. One breached right next to the boat but when I turned to see the reaction from the passengers there wasn't anyone there. They had all gone below to get out of the rain.

It's a different experience seeing whales in the rain and I rather like it. I stayed on bow watch as lookout because of the heavy fog and pouring rain and it was fun watching the waves go flat under the weight of the torrential downpour. Each drop left a little pockmark in the surface. It isn't cold today and I really enjoyed it out here.

We hung around on the banks watching whales for a while and then motored back to Gloucester. We arrived after dark, in another downpour, and rafted up with the *Adventure*. Life doesn't get boring on a schooner!

South along the Coast

August 21, Wednesday

The rain pounding on the deck woke me up this morning. The plan was to leave here by 1000, when Rich got back from the Cape. He will take command of the *Harvey* again and Eben will go home to Clinton, Connecticut, for a while. Everything went as planned and we spent the afternoon on Stellwaggon watching lots of whales in the rain.

Ruth is seasick again so I did dishes for her with the help of one of the passengers.

We are now anchored in Marblehead, and Barrett, the naturalist from the aquarium in Boston, has gone ashore for the evening so I'm setting up the equipment for her evening program, a "Save the Whales" film.

Steve, a new crew member, will be running the tender for the first time tonight and when we filled the gas tanks one of them had a tiny pinprick hole that shot gas out like a squirt gun. We tipped the tank up and plugged the tiny hole with soap to stop the leak temporarily. Some of the gas was siphoned out and as soon as the rest is used up we'd better get rid of this tank.

August 22, Thursday

At 0600 Rich knocked at our door. By 0630 we were underway in pea soup fog and motoring out to the banks. Radar is awesome. We could see not only the coast line, but every buoy, island and obstacle around us. We laid out a course line to the loran coordinates of the last place we had been finding whales. We motored through the fog sounding the fog horn every two minutes. When we got out to the banks we could hear people talking, engines running, and fog horns all around us but we couldn't make out anything through the haze.

We felt our way very slowly, watching the radar, with two bow lookouts. When we came to the place on the loran where we had seen whales before, the engine was cut and we drifted in and out of fog patches. This is a different experience being out here in the fog. Everyone's senses are tuned to a finer pitch, looking and listening for anything. We could hear whales blowing and splashing all around us, but we couldn't see them.

About 1130 the sun finally burned the fog off and as it lifted we could see that we were in the middle of a sizeable fleet of boats, all drifting around us.

There were whales all over! At one time I counted seven of them right close by. Three of them got too close for my comfort and would come right at us and then dive under the boat.

As I was the one that had taken the jib topsail off for Hurricane Bob I got to hank it back on. In order to do this I had to climb way out on the bowsprit again, watching the show the whales were putting on with one eye and hanking on the jib with the other. I noticed a light green spot moving up under the bow from way under water. As I watched it, it kept getting lighter and bigger until this huge whale came right up, broke the surface, rolled on its side so I was looking right down into its eye, and it looked at me! It was almost as if he was looking up to see what I was doing way out there on the bow. He was so close I could have put my foot down and stood on him. I had the fleeting feeling that he was going to reach up and snatch me off that bowsprit, like a bass after a fly on a branch. It all happened very quickly and then he was gone, but the picture remains in my head and I can still see that eye looking at me when I close my eyes.

The topsails are back on and I heaved a sigh of relief when the jib topsail went up without a hitch. I had hanked it on by myself, and wasn't worried about the hanks or the pennant, but leading the sheets back from the jib clew on the bow, outside everything, in the right way, was making me nervous. I had double-checked everything and told Rich it was ready, but even so I held my breath until it went up without a hitch!

We have a new cook. He doesn't like anything left on HIS saloon table and when I was called to relieve Ruth at bow watch I forgot my cup! When I came back for it, it was gone and I'm pretty sure George hid it. I'm really mad! The first cook threw my old cup out because it had a broken handle and now this new one is missing.

We're in Rockport tonight and I have tender duty again. It's a beautiful balmy night and between tender duty runs I lay on the deck and watch the stars weave back and forth through the tangle of rigging.

August 23, Friday

Up at 0600. It's sweatshirt and jacket weather again.

Rich has sailed these waters all his life and is familiar with this area. When he took a short cut through the passage between London Ledge and Thatcher Island that wasn't on the chart, I was a little concerned, but he said there was plenty of water and he'd been through here before.

There was a lady in a pink jumpsuit on Thatcher Island and when she saw us she started waving her arms over her head and jumping up and down. As we approached the narrow cut she stopped waving and just stood and watched us. We tried to figure out why she was trying to attract our attention. Was she stranded or did she have an injured person with her? Rich thought she was trying to warn us away from this very narrow danger area, and once he felt we were in safe water he was going to circle the Island and see if she needed help, and then call the CG, but once we were past the day marker on the edge of London Ledge she turned and walked away.

As we approached the banks today, we zeroed in on a whole fleet of whale watching boats and landed in a huge bunch of whales. Now it's very still and hot so I'm hiding from the sun for a while. I got sunburned yesterday and don't need any more of the high noon heat.

We're anchored in Salem tonight and as I don't have tender duty I went ashore. A bunch of us, crew and passengers, wandered around town and went into a bar called "In a Pigs Eye" but it was so crowded we couldn't get in. We moved on to a place called the "Witches Brew" which had nothing to do with witches that we could see, and after watching two guys playing darts in the back room, we moved on again. Next stop the "Chase House," which was almost civilized and quiet enough to hear each other talk. The beer here was cheap so we stayed till 2200 and caught the last tender back to the boat. My cup is back on its hook!

August 24, Saturday

It's a beautiful morning. Lots of sunshine and a nice breeze as we sailed to Boston. We were right in the middle of the racing fleet as they sailed to their starting line. We left the racing sloops at the committee boat and arrived in Boston Harbor just in time to get in line with a parade of tug boats. This is the annual push-pull contest and the harbor is full of every size tug boat imaginable. Everything from huge ocean-going tugs to a tiny one that is no bigger than my 13-foot whaler and can only seat one man. It sure is cute with its high-pitched whistle. When we pulled into the pier in Boston, Rob was waiting to take me back to New Hampshire for a week's vacation. This last trip is the end of the season out of Boston and from now on we will be working our way south. This is the last time I'll be able to have Rob pick me up until I return from the Virgin Islands this fall.

September 2, Monday

It's sunny and we are on our way south. The sail from Gloucester down to Cape Cod was beautiful with a SW wind that gave us a good point of sail and we made good time. Boston stayed off on the horizon to our right and as we got closer to the canal the traffic got a little more congested as everyone heading to Buzzard's Bay wants to catch the tide.

The coast here is much lower with long sand beaches, sandy bluffs and cliffs. We entered the canal at low slack tide and it was very simple getting in. By the time we got to the railroad bridge the tide had turned and the wind had picked up. The current was with us and carried us along at six knots, but the wind was on our nose, against the current, so we had a very choppy ride. There is no feeling of moving through the water but if you look towards the shore, it is really flying by. When we had cleared the Cleveland Ledge Light, Rich decided to spend the night in Marion. We took a right turn and are now anchored in a very quiet bay with lots of stars and an off shore breeze smelling of tidal creek.

Rich, George, and Ruth have gone to town while Charlie and I have the watch. We did 62 miles today and averaged six to seven knots. As we went through the canal it was pretty obvious that the hurricane had been through here. The trees were stripped bare and everything looks brown.

September 3, Tuesday

What a beautiful, glorious sail we had today. We are in Buzzards Bay, with all those fascinating places I've heard of like Martha's Vineyard and Woods Hole, just to name a few. The training chart that I learned navigation on is of this area and it's interesting to see the actual places and navigational aids that we used for charting.

We sailed almost to the Woods Hole entrance, then tacked and headed back towards West Island. It took all day to tack up to Cuttyhunk where we are anchored tonight. It was a great sail with the waves spraying over the front half of the boat and washing across the deck. I got a good wetting a couple of times.

We're just outside the harbor entrance as there isn't enough water in the channel to float the Harvey. This seems to be a well protected area and there are quite a few other sailboats here with us. The tide was against us this afternoon or we would have made better time so tomorrow we will leave early again as we still have 120 miles to go in two days. Hopefully we can continue to sail without the engine but if time or tide runs against us we'll have to use the auxiliary power.

With this group of 15 and 16 year old students on board we can't sail at night. Something in the contract. So we will have to take advantage of all the daylight we can get.

Sept 4, Wednesday

0500 wake-up call. The wind is still out of the SW and blowing strong. Venus is the morning star and Orion is back. He came up in the east bright and strong sometime around 0400.

We are now in the middle of Buzzards Bay on a course of 230 from Cuttyhunk to Newport, Rhode Island. It's a pretty lively ride because of the chop and I got soaked to the waist and elbows again when I was on the bow securing the staysail gasket. The water isn't even cold!

We are having another great sail even though quite a few of the kids are getting seasick. Right off our starboard bow is an old cement barge that went aground on the reef and is just sitting there almost awash. I guess it's been there a long time and even though it's not lit there is a bell buoy that's supposed to be a warning.

I like the feeling of Buzzards Bay, maybe because the water is a little warmer. We tacked three or four times and now at 1400 we're in Newport getting fuel and water. Rich has made a run uptown to pick up a chart. There are boats all over in this harbor and the entrance to Narragansett Bay is off to our right.

This is exciting being in the capitol of the racing world and I remember how badly I wanted to come here for the America's Cup races eight years ago when Rob had sent me passes to be on the USCG Chase.

Now here I am, moored to a buoy in the middle of the harbor, waiting for George the cook to return with some groceries.

We motored out of Newport with a stiff breeze right on the nose and had to power a long way out in order to clear Point Judith and be able to use our sails. Once we cleared the point we raised the three lowers and fell off on a starboard tack to Block Island.

After dinner I laid down for a while, trying to get some rest before I come on watch at 2000-midnight. The waves slapped the hull occasionally but most of the time it was a smooth ride. I dozed off and on but there was the whole gang of kids in the saloon laughing and carrying on which made it a little hard to sleep. I must have fallen asleep finally and no one called me for the 2000 watch as there were all kinds of people on deck enjoying the sail to Block Island. The buoy on the north end of Block Island seems to be off station according to the loran and radar, but Charlie turned wide of it anyway and we tacked back towards the mainland. The seas seem to have settled down some so I finally fell asleep and had a good rest.

September 5, Thursday

At 0400 Rich woke me up for the 0400 - 0800 watch, and advised me to dress for wet weather. He wasn't kidding because as we approached the entrance to Long Island Sound it was pouring!

When we passed the light house on the tip of Long Island about an hour after the tide had turned, we had a six knot current pushing us along with the flood. We met three 200-meter tug-and-tow rigs and one huge freighter riding the last of the ebb tide through the "race." After that there wasn't any more east bound traffic. Too much current to fight.

We passed through what is called the "race" without any problems as we had the current with us. There was lots and lots of heavy rain, and some fairly close thunder and lighting, but by 0600 it started to lighten up and finally slowed down to a drizzle. The shoreline, with all its city and town lights and all the navigation buoys and light houses, would be shining clear and easy to identify, and then in a torrential squall everything would be wiped out. A comforting feeling though is the fact that when we could see the lights they were where they were supposed to be, and that is always nice on a dark stormy morning.

I came back on watch at noon and there was still a light drizzle but it was much warmer and actually kind of nice. The wind shifted around to the north and we had a smooth, swift ride right to the entrance to Norwalk.

Instead of going into town we are anchored out here by an island with the ruins of what looks like a very fancy home, and will stay here tonight. The leaders of this group are afraid to turn 30 junior high school kids loose at the festival. After breakfast we'll head into Norwalk and dock around noon. Rich was worried about being late and we are actually a little early.

This has been quite a trip, The Ernestina was supposed to have half these kids, but when her prop broke we got then all. Right now we have a boat-load of hyperactive teenagers that are all screaming and jumping off the rig into the water. I hope the swim wears them out.

This is very pretty in here with lots of neat little lighthouses on the outlying shoals and islands. The water isn't very deep or clean but there are some nice sandy beaches.

September 6, Friday

We got up early again and Rich, George, and Charlie, along with the chaperons, had the kids pack up all their belongings and clean their cabins. What a lot of fuss. It took about two hours but finally everything was stuffed into bags and brought on deck.

After breakfast we motored the last stretch into town through a very narrow, winding channel with rocks and shoals on both sides. The Oysterfest committee wasn't quite ready for us so we hung off two buoys, bow and stern, so we wouldn't swung into the channel. Again we had to use the tender to off board the kids.

We had some time to kill before our spot was ready as there were oyster boats unloading huge baskets of oysters on the dock. We used the time to clean the ship. One sheet on each bunk with a folded blanket at the foot, and the bunks look presentable. We will have a lot of people wandering through the boat in the next couple of days and the bunks look better when they're made up.

At 1500 we got the okay to come in and just as we were approaching our landing, Dan, the cook, came around the corner with his family and friends. Just in time to catch our lines.

Dan has been on vacation for the last week and I'm glad he's back. His dad, who had been on the Nova Scotia trip with us, and his dad's wife brought Dan back to the boat and will stay around for the festival.

Rich and I were invited to Muffy's (one of the chaperons) home for showers. They have a beautiful home with a lovely big yard full of old trees and flower gardens. We sat out in the garden under an old copper beech tree on white wrought iron chairs and had ice cold beer and little round pieces of garlic toast. Lovely.

At 1900 we took a boat load of people out for a cruise in Long Island sound, but as there was no wind all we could do was raise the sails and motor out, cut the engine and drift.

We got back here at 2130 and Rich, Charlie and George the cook took the tender and ran over to the Oysterfest. Dan, George and I stayed here, had a peanut butter sandwich, and called it a night.

September 7, Saturday

The weather has been beautiful and so far we've done two "dude" cruises. These consist of loading all kinds of people on the boat, going out into the river to raise the sails, and then motoring out into the sound. Then, because there is no wind, the engine is cut to give the effect of sailing, and we drift for a while. No one seems to notice as they are along for the drinks and conversation. After a little bit, we head back in to lower and stow the sails, tie up at the dock and off board the passengers. This would probably be more interesting if we had some wind. The second cruise was catered and they left all kinds of pop and beer behind.

I was on watch tonight and three local sailors that have a yawl at the next dock stopped by to admire the boat. It was lucky they were there because as we they were looking around and I made the rounds with them, we discovered the tender being forced under the water by the rising tide. She had her bow under the dock and the stern was starting to rise out of the water. The tide had caught her and was slowly forcing her bow under. I couldn't have got her out myself but the three guys got on board, got way up on the bow, and their combined weight was enough to let them push her back out till she popped up like a cork. I invited them along for the 1100 "cruise" the next morning.

After they left I sat on deck and watched the festival going on across the river. Swarms of people milling around and the smell of greasy food drifting across the river to me along with the sounds of a couple of noisy bands playing. I haven't been over there yet and probably won't go either.

September 8, Sunday

Another hot, clear, sunny day. Very little wind, but we did three "dude" cruises today. What a bother! I'd hate to do this kind of charter all the time but it helps pay some of the expenses and is good exposure. The three guys that helped me with the boat last night came aboard and as they sail around here all the time they are familiar with the area. They showed us a different channel and it made the trip a little more interesting as we circumnavigated a couple of islands and got some of the history of the place. This is very low lying land and the channels are mostly tidal, so when the tide is out we wouldn't have enough water to float the Harvey going this way, but it was interesting and gave us some new scenery to look at.

I volunteered to stay aboard again tonight so the rest of the crew could go to the festival. I really don't like all the noise and people and would rather watch from a distance. I didn't have to twist any arms.

Two of the guys that had been on the cruise with us (can't remember their names) stopped by to invite me for a sail on their yawl. That would have been fun but we leave for Mystic Seaport in the morning.

September 9, Monday

Hot, sunny, still. George the cook and George the crew went to New York last night and George the crew isn't back as yet. George the cook brought back some enormous muffins, the biggest I've ever seen. They were delicious, and came from the train station in New York.

An oyster boat tied up alongside because we won't be leaving until 1100 on the flood tide. They have 15 big metal baskets just full of oysters, starfish, and a lot of un-nameable things that were dredged from the bottom of the sound with the oysters. A big fat sea gull is strutting around on the top of the heap picking out whatever looks good to him. He just ate a long white worm that is wiggling frantically even as it's being swallowed. The oyster boats are pretty; they have low wide hulls and on the stern are cranes with big metal scoops that open their jaws to take a bite out of the bottom and bring up everything they find there.

We took down all the signal flags and Pepsi pennants that had been "dressing" the ship. The string of lights that had been strung from the bow up to the top of the masts and down to the stern had to be taken back down and packed carefully away. Charlie went to the top of the main while Rich went to the top of the fore and they lowered them down to us waiting on the deck. All the pop and beer cans that had been stuck in corners all over the deck were found and trashed and she is starting to look like a working vessel again.

At 1100 we got underway with the ebb tide and headed back NE. I thought I could work on some sewing projects on the trip to Mystic as there were no passengers, but instead we took all the life jackets and spread them out to air. Then George and I went into each cabin, took the water spigot off its holder, sanded the holder, gave it a coat of paint and after that dried, replaced the spigot.

The tide has turned and we weren't making any headway so now we are anchored off Clinton, Conn. This is where Eben lives, but I can't make out anything on shore.

For the next 6 hours I'm on watch. At 0115 I'll wake Rich and the crew. I volunteered for this job and it's very nice sitting out here watching the sound. There isn't much traffic because of the foul current (everyone heading down has gone by and everyone else is waiting for the tide to turn, like us) and it's very quiet and peaceful. The deal we made was if I take this all night watch alone and let the rest of the crew sleep, I could sleep the rest of the night and they would bring the boat in. Rich needs to get as much sleep as possible whenever he can and he will have to be on deck to bring the boat into Mystic in the morning.

At 1150 we started to swing at anchor as the tide began to slack. The wind is out of the NE and it fascinates me to watch the effect of the wind, tides and currents on the hull of a boat. Even though the wind is blowing us down, the current has more control of the hull and it is pushing us up against the wind.

We had been given bushels of oysters and clams in Norwalk and this afternoon some of them were prepared on deck so everyone could enjoy them. I had a couple and they weren't too bad but the clams are rather chewy and tough. I could live without either raw oysters or clams and won't miss them at all.

September 10, Tuesday: Mystic Seaport

This is a real treat to be in Mystic, tied to the same pier as the "Henry Morgan" and being part of the Museum. There is a definite feeling of being in the 16th century with all the period costumes and props around the dock. Some of our crew look like they belong here with their long hair and beards. The costumes the staff wear on the Morgan are the regular working clothes of the schooner sailor - apparently that hasn't changed for hundreds of years and is traditional.

I made a quick run over to the yarn shop after lunch and they have a lot of nautical needlepoint so I'll have to go back.

September 11, Wednesday

The showers here are beautiful! There is a large building that is built to look like the New York yacht club and the facilities are great. From the window over the sinks the view is of the Mystic River and some of the museum grounds.

It's just a short walk back to the boat past a changing assortment of transiting sailboats that have come in for the night on their travels. The weather is beautiful and after breakfast we painted all day.

After dinner we washed clothes and then lay out on the deck to watch the stars until bedtime.

September 13, Friday

Painted the sole in "Margaret." Went to Providence, R.I., for drug test for my application for officer. We'll be here for three weeks doing Elderhostel.

September 14, Saturday

There is to be a wedding on board today: One of the people that used to work on the boat is getting married so Eben let him use the boat. We swabbed the decks and did a general clean up and then moved over to a dock by downtown Mystic. Rich let Charlie run the boat and he didn't do too bad a job - at least he didn't hit anything. We had a long throw with the heaving lines and warped her in. Not too bad for the first time; this is a big boat.

While the wedding was going on Gail and I walked up-town Mystic to wash clothes and explore a little.

We have some new shipmates. Gail is from Chicago and has worked with the new cook George; even if she hasn't had any sailing experience she was hired because of her restaurant background and George's recommendation. She is bunking with me now that Ruth has left. She is a neat person and learns fast.

Gregg is our newest crew and will probably be the first mate. He has a Captain's license also and was on a farm in Maine for the summer but decided that the Virgin Islands was the place to be for the winter.

Dave is only 20 but has worked on the Harvey before and also worked on the "Bill of Rights." He is very quiet but seems to know his job.

Charlie is gone; we gave him a copy of "The Hobbit" that everyone signed - he has never read it! He will be missed.

We brought the boat back to the museum dock after the wedding, then the whole gang went to "The Seamen's Pub" for happy hour. It was 0200 before we got back to the boat and Gregg heard that there wouldn't be any coffee in the morning because the stove blower was broken! I located the spare blower in the lazaret and we replaced it before we went to bed.

September 15, Sunday

I got up at 0800 and lit the stove - it works, but it's sure temperamental. At least I got the coffee made and then someone requested hot Quaker oats. Then Dan spoke up from his hole in the corner of the saloon requesting scrambled eggs with cheese - in bed yet! He got his request, too.

It started to pour so we put the awning up over the main deck and then cleaned the cabins and put fresh sheets on all the bunks.

We boarded 26 Elderhostel in the rain and after getting them settled, I hit the sack exhausted at 2000.

September 16, Monday

The *Henry Morgan*, a 200-year-old whaling boat from the New Bedford fleet, had all its new sails run out this morning for a picture taking session. They have been working on a new set of sails for her for quite a while and want to have then all finished for her birthday promotion. Every sail was set in the calm of the dawn but when I took the second boat load of passengers out in the river to get some shots of the whole ship, the wind suddenly started to pick up and the Henry Morgan started to pull at her tether. The chain that was holding her to the land had been buried in the muck at the bottom of the river for a long time but with this wind she pulled so hard the chain came up taut at the surface. All kinds of seaweed and junk were exposed to the sunlight before the sails were down and under control. The Henry Morgan settled back in her berth and I could almost hear her sigh.

All the passengers spent the day at the museum as part of the educational program for the week, so after the heavy weekend we got the day off to explore. I wandered all over Mystic and went into each and every building. The sun came out and it's gotten hot and very muggy. At 1400 I went to the planetarium and took in the navigation program. Interesting.

I'm now the official purser with a pay raise.

Sept. 17, Tuesday

At 0700 we left the museum to make the 0715 bridge opening at downtown Mystic. The river is beautiful with lots of unique and pretty houses lining the banks and miles of sailboats at their moorings. It was very hazy as we left and when we got into Long Island Sound I was reminded of the Maine fog.

The breeze freshened and the seas started to build so we had a good ride.

Things really got interesting as we sailed through a narrow channel into the great salt pond in Block Island. Again we didn't head up to drop the sails, I'm not sure why, but we dropped them running off the wind and it was a real Chinese fire drill with this new crew. No one was sure what position they were supposed to be responsible for so as a result we had at least three "in charge" people giving different orders. We did get them down and secured and then got ready to drop the hook. The crew was a little disgruntled to say the least with all the mixed orders coming from everyone but the Captain.

After setting the hook and letting out 200 feet of chain, we had a large cruise ship pull in and pick up its mooring. It seems we are too close to him now and as this is his permanent mooring we have to move. After pulling the anchor, which was good practice for the new crew, we tied up at the dock.

The galley pump won't pump anymore; it has been getting slower and slower drawing water and it finally gave up. Seeing as I can't make it any worse I've volunteered to fix it. The leather gasket was shot and after that was replaced it works pretty well except the shaft of the pump is pretty rusty and pock marked.

Gail and I took about a four-mile hike out to the point on the SW side of the island and found a beautiful sand beach overlooking the sound. Block Island is beautiful; lots of big rustic homes with split log and rock fences, rolling hills, ponds and pine trees. A smaller schooner ghosted in last night and set its hook out in the pond. It has an interesting profile.

September 18, Wednesday
The schooner pulled into the dock this morning to fuel up and it is a steel hulled boat going north for repairs. I talked to the owner and we exchanged business cards and tours of the boats. He claims to be "like the *Flying Dutchman*."

We left the salt pond on Block Island and headed out into the sound. The seas are old and choppy but at least the fog has lifted and we can see Montauk Point and the Connecticut coast. We put the sails up in the salt pond and sailed out through the very narrow channel, past the Coast Guard station, where some of the Coasties were out working on a boat. We had a quiet and relaxing sail across the sound to Watch Hill where we are tied up for the night.

The dock fees here are only $25.00 whereas last night at Block Island they charged us $1.00 a foot! That adds up real quick when you're a 95-foot schooner.

The town of Stonington is very old and quaint - narrow streets and well-taken-care-of buildings. I like this town better than some we have been in. I found an old book store in a private home, and bought a big thick, old book full of sea stories for only $8.00. I also found a set of "Pup. 229" for celestial navigation. Greg wants to brush up on his celestial and all his books and equipment got burned in some fire.

The fog and rain closed in just at sunset and now the wind is building and pushing us hard against the dock.

September 19, Thursday

Cloudy, but no fog. We started the day by warping the boat back 200 feet along the dock. We were being blown hard against the dock and the only way off was to warp the boat down to the end, slide around the corner and then power off. It took about two and a half hours using spring lines, lots of fenders, and the engine. The wind was so strong the dock actually bent where we were pushed against it.

The cathead, a long beam that extends out from the ship just aft of the bow, kept getting hung up on the dock posts. After a couple of yells about the cat being fouled and we would have to stop and readjust the spring lines, one of the guests suggested we put the cat below decks so it wouldn't get in the way anymore.

We finally got underway with only a little paint left behind and set sail. There were some beautiful swells and we took water over the cap rails a couple of times. We were having fun until a front moved in with some good gusts and lots of rain. Things got a little interesting for a while and the water hitting us in the face was a mixture of salt and fresh from the sea spray and the torrential rain.

We navigated a very winding channel with shoals, rocks and sandbars into Gardiners Bay. Greg got on the radio to the harbor master and got permission to use the dock directly across from the harbor entrance.

We could use the dock but he forgot to tell us that there wasn't enough water to float this boat! We went aground about 10 feet from the end of the dock but the bottom was soft so all we did was to come to a gentle standstill. The wind was on the stern though so we would have to move fast or be blown down into a real stuck situation. The tender was launched and Dave started pushing the bow out. This didn't work so the Danforth anchor was carried out and dropped so we could kedge off with that. This worked and we picked the anchor up on the way out to deeper water. We are now outside the breakwater at Sag Harbor in 15 feet of water and anchored for the night. It is very dark, cold and wet with rain and wind beating on the boat. The guests are watching "Captains Courageous" and Greg and I are cleaning up after a late but delicious turkey dinner.

September 20, Friday

It's still raining and there's a cold wind out of the NE. The deck is shipshape and as we motor past Cedar Point out towards Gardiners Bay we are heading right into the wind and current. We will push between Plum Island and Orient Point .This is "The Race": one of the notorious places that have a bad reputation for rip tides. The tide will be slack in another hour so hopefully if we make some headway we can make the passage at slack tide and be into Long Island Sound. There is a terrific tidal current in here as the tide ebbs and flows and the channel isn't very wide so I hope the timing is right and we have enough power to get through. Kind of like trying to cross the river without getting pushed downstream.

It's cold and wet and dreary but the crew is starting to work well together and I think we will really get to be a team.

We crossed the race through a narrow cut between Orient Point and Plum Island and I thought it was really ripping, but some of the natives kept trying to tell me that it was calm and gets a lot worse. We didn't have enough horsepower to push against the current so we tacked almost to Plum Island, then tacked again and motor sailed through.

We tacked back and forth off New London for a couple of hours but as the tide was setting in the wrong direction and we weren't making any head way Rich turned the engine on and we motor sailed into Mystic. We arrived at the dock at 1700 as the sun came out but it's still very cold.

Virginia stopped by again and took me to her friend's cabin on the beach at Greatneck by Niantic. This is beautiful; right on the beach overlooking Long Island sound with big rocks surrounding a strip of crescent shaped sand beach. I'm constantly amazed at the beauty of the areas I've been in. New York was supposed to be just a big city and Long Island Sound like a river running through the middle. But there are lots of wild areas and farm land . Geography should be taught this way. After a long hot shower we went into Niantic for dinner: sauteed scallops in garlic and wine sauce.

We got back to the boat by 2200 and called it a day.

September 21, Saturday

Woke up to a bright, cold, crisp day. We got the cabins all washed and clean but had to wait for Eben to show up with the sheets before we could finish. Gail and I did the crew laundry and stopped for coffee at a little outside cafe down a side street in Mystic. We had a whole cart load of laundry and must have looked like a couple of bag ladies - or boat people.

When we got back to the boat we finished up a few odd jobs and now we're waiting for a video called "Mystic Pizza." Dan and Michelle, a friend of Eben's, have gone to pick it up in her car. It was a very unique and enjoyable evening. Everyone except Rich and George the cook stayed here on the boat. We made popcorn and watched the movie. This is the first time that I remember that everyone didn't split and go their separate ways on a Saturday night. This is really nice and I'm glad this is the group that will be taking the boat south because we all seem to get along and work together very well.

It is cold! We lit the stove and closed all the skylights to make it cozy in here but once we turned the stove off for the night the cold moved in very fast. Almost a full moon and there is a brilliant display of stars tonight.

September 22, Sunday

Greg cooked breakfast and although the morning was supposed to be free there were lots of things that needed doing before our guests arrived at 1400. Therefore I never got off the ship except to run over to the store for a navigation tool. I also picked up a book, "Folklore and the Sea."

I got a chance to wear shorts for about two hours today and then it turned cold again. All the guests have reported aboard except two and now the saloon is full of people playing bridge. Looks like everyone is staying aboard again tonight.

September 23, Monday

Full Moon and the fall equinox. Rain this morning and showers all day. The guests have gone to a series of lectures at the museum so I got a chance to make a trip to the museum research library and finally found the "Ballad of the *Flying Dutchman*."

This afternoon we (Gail, Dan, Dave, Greg, and I) went to New London to shop at the Salvation Army and the military discount stores. I got a pair of bell bottoms, military issue, and everyone seems to think they are hilarious. Greg picked up a Greek sailing hat with a merchant marine pin on the crown, which he claims is his symbol of rank as an officer.

George and I have the dishes tonight and then I have watch. The moon is starting to peek out occasionally and it would sure be nice to have sun to sail with tomorrow.

September 24, Tuesday

Left Mystic at 0800 to make the town lift bridge and the swinging railroad bridge. It was a quiet sail and we are now tied at the dock in Newport, Rhode Island. I walked the town strip and after dinner we had a sea chantey singer from the Mystic museum give us a concert right here on deck. Geoffrey (Jeff) is one of the leaders for this week's cruise, and now we are sitting here, on the deck of the

Harvey, in downtown Newport harbor, listening to sea chanteys and ballads sung with guitar, flute, and concertina accompaniment. What could be better?

We are expecting squalls; 50 knot winds are predicted for Narragansett Bay. We have rigged double hawsers. It doesn't look bad yet.

September 25, Wednesday

We had a fairly quiet night; some rain but not much wind. Just when we figured the storm wasn't going to hit us it started to blow for real. Rich and Greg had left for a "conference" - since Greg has been given the job of first mate he's become a real pain and is causing all kinds of problems with the crew. Rich took him off for a while to talk.

After watching the big awning billow a couple of times we decided to take it down. Then we added another hawser out the starboard hawse hole and led it forward to some solid pilings on land. Everything else we were tied to was part of a floating dock and that didn't look too secure. We were putting chaffing gear on the fender boards when Rich and Greg showed up so now we had all kinds of help.

We spent the day here at Newport riding out the squall.

September 26, Thursday

We woke up to low, racing black clouds and a wind shift into the north. We'll make a run for Block Island but will have to motor out until we clear the land at Point Judith. The swells kept getting bigger and bigger till an estimate was made at six to seven feet.

The swells are far apart so although we go way up and down the motion is easy and we don't take any water on the deck. It's raining off and on and very cold so everyone is in full foul weather gear. Because it is so dark with limited visibility, we also have the navigation lights on - all in all it's a pretty miserable run across the sound in the rain, cold and uncomfortable. A CG helicopter and a 44-footer are working the area. There's report that a helicopter went down somewhere around here and they are still looking for it.

We got into the salt pond at Block Island around noon and the sun came out. It's still very brisk but I guess that is to be expected at the end of September.

We all worked on the ship until 1600, and then had the rest of the evening off. The guests went ashore to explore, but the island is almost all closed down. It goes from 20,000 in the summer to less than 800 for the winter.

Parked next to us is a yawl built of ferrous cement. I went over to talk to the couple that is aboard and they told me they had started to build this boat 17 years ago back in the Canadian brush. He had exact measurements for getting it through the railroad tunnels and down to the St. Lawrence River when it was ready to launch.

They got this far on their dream trip south and although they have a fantastic selection of navigation equipment - loran, GPS, radar, and both a marine radio and a SSB - they have not sailed the boat. So far all they've done is motor and they are looking for crew to teach them and help sail her. They have motored all the way and are using too much diesel. Now they are heading for New York and Cape May, and after that it will be all the way in the Inland waterway. He wanted me to talk to his wife as apparently we are about the same age and if I could do it so could she.

It's a beautiful clear night, with an almost full moon and lots of stars.

September 27, Friday
Sunny, cold, and a light wind in here. We head back to Mystic today.

We had a beautiful sail with blue skies and big white puffy clouds, nice wind even though we had to tack from Block Island out towards Montauk Point and then back to Fisher's Island. It was a great sail and we had all seven sails flying. We got back to the Mystic River entrance in time to make the railroad bridge but missed the drawbridge in Mystic so we had to tie up to some pilings along the river bank for about half an hour until it opened.

As we passed through the open drawbridge, Eben was standing on the bridge with a lot of other people and waved at us.

It's clear and cold tonight but the stars are great. Eben is on board and I think Rich has left for the weekend. We also have a lot of guests that will spend the night aboard and leave in the morning but they have all gone to bed. Some of the crew went to get a video. I'm sitting here with the saloon to myself and a mug of HOT southern comfort in my hand, catching up with my log - nice!

Tomorrow we start the clean up and change over and on Monday we leave for the Chesapeake. I don't know if we will be going up the Delaware from Cape May and then through the C&D canal to Annapolis or all the way down around Cape Charles and then up the Chesapeake to Annapolis, but either way will be interesting.

September 28, Saturday

Another sunny, cool day. We spent the morning cleaning cabins and the afternoon washing crew clothes. Eben was here and left about 4 p.m. after water proofing the canvas. We have a new midshipman, and Dutch came on board with his buddy. We now have two official Captains and lots of very strong personalities fighting for supremacy. This should be very interesting to say the least. I'm beginning to feel like I'm in never-never land and we have a bunch of Peter Pans trying to prove how great they are.

Most of the crew has gone to New London bar hopping I'm but staying on the boat for the evening. It's cold out and all the hatches are closed and the stove is lit. It's nice and cozy in here with the radio playing and the stove keeping us warm. I'm on watch tonight and tried to make popcorn again but this time it burned. I poured the melted butter on Cheerios and that tasted just as good.

Tomorrow we have the day off and on Monday we leave for the Chesapeake.

September 29, Sunday

We're still in Mystic Seaport and the river is covered with drifting fog this morning. It's beautiful and the trees are starting to get that fall look. It's very crisp and cool and I took a long hot shower and steamed up the whole room. Then Gail and I walked into town and sat in the sun right on the bank of the river to watch the ships pass by. I did some cross stitching and then went back to the boat. What a beautiful fall day!

I mailed the application for the upgrade in my license today as I'd gotten the drug test results and my current physical. The gentleman at the Mystic book store was nice and made copies for me.

We have our Chesapeake Captain aboard; he wears a long army great coat with pins and medals on the lapel; one is the CG coxswain pin. He was in the CG for four years and ran a rescue boat on the Chesapeake out of Annapolis so should know his way around down there.

Rich will be the Captain on the trip down and it looks like we will have lots of very qualified crew!

September 30, Monday

We're on our way! After spending the better part of the day running around doing last minute errands and taking on water, ice, and groceries, we finally left in time to catch the 4:15 highway bridge opening at Mystic. It is cold but we have enough crew to do a three watch schedule which will be four hours on and eight hours off.

We cleared the railroad bridge and wound our way down river with lots of people waving goodbye. We even got a cannon salute from the "Brilliant" as we went past her. We ate dinner while underway and then our watch went down for a nap as we're on the 2000 to midnight watch.

When I came on deck at 2000 the navigation lights were already on and it was starting to get dark but as the stars came out it never really got dark and it was almost like a moonlit night. We could see the horizon it was so bright with starlight.

The wind is cold and brisk but there isn't enough of it to move the boat very well so we are motor sailing and the boat is very gently lifting and bobbing through the swells with an occasional spray of white that comes over the cap rail when we catch a wave just right

We have passed between Block Island and Mohegan Point at the top of Long Island and are heading out into the North Atlantic. At 2300 the light houses of Mohegan and Block Island disappeared over the edge of the horizon and all we could see is the flash as they sent out their signals.

At midnight we changed course to 240 which will take us way off shore and out past the Ambrose Light. This will put us on a straight line to the Cape May entrance to the Delaware.

Then the moon came up just forward of our beam like a fire on the horizon. At first it was just a faint orange glow and then as it grew I could see the half moon floating on its back as it crept up into the sky. The big dipper is almost dipping the lower edge of its cup into the water and the stars are spectacular. We are making 7.2 knots according to the walker log that we put over at 2300 but the loran doesn't give us credit for that much speed so maybe we have a foul current that is slowing our distance over the ground . Regardless, the sailing and the night are beautiful and the boat feels alive and is handling well.

October 1, Tuesday

I had the 0800 to noon watch this morning and it was pretty quiet. Not a lot of wind; sunny and warm. After lunch I got the sextants out and drew a crowd - everyone tried looking through them but from the conversations it's pretty obvious that they need more background in basic navigation before they can move onto celestial. They all enjoyed being able to use the sextant anyway.

At 1500 I went below to take a nap and woke up when the boat was tacked. The waves and wind have picked up and it's getting pretty wild out here. We were even taking water over the bow cap rails and while I was on watch from 1800 to 2000 I was stationed on the bow as lookout. The water would spray high and pick up the green and red colors from the navigation lights. I was wedged between the sampson posts on the bowsprit and it was exhilarating. Rich came forward and asked me to finish the watch back by the break in the deck. I guess it was wilder up there than I realized and I even had some water in my jacket pocket so maybe it wasn't as safe as I thought.

0200 – early morning, Wednesday

I go on watch again at 0400 and I'm sitting in my cabin bouncing up and down. I guess if it's this bumpy down here amidships it's pretty rough topside.

October 2, Wednesday

I took a short nap and then back up at 0340 for the 0400 - 0800 watch. It's a beautiful brilliant starlit night and Orion is up and all tangled in the starboard rigging. What a thrill to look up at Orion through the ratlines and rigging of a gaff-rigged schooner! We are under sail off the New Jersey coast with a fair rolling sea without much wind. We still get an occasional spray over the decks but everything has become pretty quiet.

There is a ship's light way off in the distance that hasn't moved for a couple of hours, and a chopper that keeps circling the area. We think they might be doing some kind of night practice maneuvers. When the sun came up they were both gone.

I took a couple of sun shots after breakfast and then took a nap. Sunshine and warmth. I slept till my 1600 watch and now there are signs of bad weather coming - one huge ring around the sun, and sun dogs on both sides. After dinner the 1600 - 1800 dog watch gets to do the dishes so Jim and I did these (we have a lot of new temporary crew for the passage) and then I went back to bed till 2330 when we were called to drop the main. At 2400 I went on watch till 0400 and the bad weather hasn't happened yet. I came on deck dressed for squalls and ended up in shirt sleeves. It was a warm, grey velvet night with just a little wind and long lazy swells. Atlantic City was looming on our starboard beam and there were bright white lights of fishing boats dotting the ocean around us. At 0230 we spotted the Racon buoy which marks the entrance to Delaware Bay and just as our watch was over it started to rain.

I took the walker log in before I went below but even being very careful to feed the bitter end back into the water to untangle it I managed to get a snarl that took 20 minutes to untangle. The algae in our wake seem to be whiter and greener here then the blue of Mystic and Maine. Then back to bed.

October 3, Thursday

Stuck my head out at 0800 and everyone on watch is in foul weather gear in the rain, light swells, and poor visibility. We are entering the Delaware but can't see any land. Back to bed as I'm on watch again at noon to 1600 and then after two dog watches our team has the 2000 to midnight. This is the "swing day" where our watch has three four- hour watches in a row. I guess today won't be much good for anything but sleeping and standing watch.

This cabin is a cocoon of sound. The engine is right next door so its purr muffles just about everything else. There isn't any wind now and as the boat rocks in the gentle swells I can hear the swish of the ocean as it goes past the hull next to my bunk. There will be an occasional clanking as the foresail sheets slide back and forth in the gentle breeze and the radio can be heard occasionally with someone calling. There isn't much radio traffic out here as there aren't very many boats around. I can't hear any voices over these noises and except for an occasional footstep overhead and the blocking of the light when someone steps on the deck prism, I could be alone on the boat.

1600 and I just got off watch, had a short shower, and then the sun came out. The bay has gone flat glassy calm and we're almost to the Ship John Shoal light house. Four hours to take a nap and get dinner out of the way and we're back on watch. We should be in the C&D canal by that time and maybe into the upper Chesapeake. I don't know if we will stop in Chesapeake city for the night or push right on to Annapolis. It's very hot! What a change from Connecticut and Maine.

As I came on deck for the 2000 to midnight watch we were just approaching the entrance to the C&D canal. It was dusk and a HUGE ship was coming out from under the bridge. We did a slow 360-degree turn to let him clear the canal and pass us. As we approached the bridge "Buddy" shot the cannon and we struck our colors just as we passed under it. We have plenty of clearance to go under here but it still looks like we will scrape the bottom of the bridge as we go through.

The lights are very overwhelming after the open water. There is a yellow street light every 100 feet along both shores, and when the canal curves it looks like there is no way out as the outside bank has the same yellow lights. We are screaming along at seven knots with the ebb tide and it is very nerve wracking and I'm not even at the helm.

At 2000 our watch takes over and I'm on bow watch for the first hour so I have a chance to adjust to the lights before I have to take the helm.

Another huge ship is coming up the channel towards us and he is so big and the lights are so high and far apart that I lose him in the background. I tried to see without the binoculars and he blocks the whole left side of the channel

At 2100 I took the helm just in time to make the run under the bridge at Chesapeake City. A nice curve as we approach and then a bend to the left. Now we are away from all the yellow lights and have the flashing red and green buoy markers to follow. There is another huge ship that passed us and I'd swear there wasn't room in the channel for him, much less both of us. Talk about close encounters!

Out in the upper Bay the lights are less intimidating and the channel markers are good targets to aim at. We also have range lights to help keep us in the channel so I think it's a lot easier.

At 2200 I'm back on bow watch and I spot some lights down channel. They look big even at this distance and there is a lot of space between the bow lights. As we get closer the lights get higher and higher and the black hull disappears in the dark. The only way I know where that ship is, is by watching as this big black hole "eats" the shore lights as it passes between us and the shoreline.

It has small porthole lights showing, and those along with the range lights and the red navigation light way up overhead make it look a space ship. Soon the whole shoreline is gone and then they pass with a quiet and sinister swishing until all we see are the stern lights.

It's a beautiful balmy night without much breeze and there is an incredible amount of flashing and blinking, red, white and green lights all over the bay. Added to all the lights on shore we have a real confusion of light.

"Dutch," who will be the Captain for this section of charters, is in his home cruising grounds and is the pilot for this run down the bay in the middle of the night. Otherwise I think we would have stayed over in Chesapeake City and made this part of the trip in the morning. When my watch ended at 2400 I was going to stay up but changed my mind.

October 4, Friday

At 0600 I woke up and wrote these last few pages and just now as I stuck my head up through the hatch I saw the double Chesapeake bridges behind us so we are almost in Annapolis. Breakfast soon and then we'll probably drop a hook.

We are anchored right in front of the Naval Academy and after squaring things up a boat load of us went to town and I had a beautiful shower. Gail and I walked around town for a while and then I came back to the boat. It's a pretty quiet time and everyone is sort of hanging around or doing errands.

Everyone is a little tired from the passage. We left at 1600 on Monday and arrived here on Friday morning - 88 hours underway and most of it with the engine on because we had very little wind.

It's warm here and tomorrow we will clean the boat for Sunday, when we board an Elderhostel group for a week's cruise on the Chesapeake.

October 5, Saturday

A beautiful fall day. The Annapolis Cadets were up bright and early this morning running around the football fields. We pulled the anchor and went over to the fuel dock. Here Rich left and gave me a big hug; he will be back in three weeks when he'll relieve Dutch for the next segment of the passage.

We motored out of the harbor along with the Saturday morning race committee boats and racing fleet. This harbor is a zoo! We motored out into the bay until we cleared the buoy off Bloody Point where we set sail and had a beautiful beam reach at eight and a half knots for about an hour. Then we had to turn the corner into the wind to get to St. Michael's so the motor came on and the sails were stowed.

St Michael's looks like a nice place even though the channel in is very snaky and not very deep. We are tied to the end of the pier and there are two huge bells and a cannon right next to us. This is a maritime museum and I'm going to look around tomorrow. There are lots of neat classic wooden boats but tonight I'm on watch so the exploring will have to wait.

Greg, the first mate, claims it doesn't take two people to do the ship's laundry - all you do is fill the machines, read a magazine, throw the stuff in a dryer and come home. I asked him if it was so easy why didn't he do it and show us how simple it really is. He bit and is doing the wash! He is really mad, though, so I pulled my stuff out and will wash it myself tomorrow; I'm afraid he might have an "accident" with something of mine. Four hours later Greg showed up and dumped sacks of unfolded laundry in the saloon and claimed he won the bet. I didn't know what the bet was or that we had one going but he didn't complain when two of the crew went to do the laundry after that. And he didn't volunteer. Eben wanted to know how I ever talked him into doing the laundry.

October 6, Sunday

I got up at 0600 and took a nice shower. I figured by noon everything would be done and I could explore for a couple of hours. There are only three bunks left to clean and then the passengers won't board until 1730 this afternoon.

High tide is supposed to be at 0931 so at that time we planned to move the boat but at 0937 we are stuck! We had a lot of discussion about when the next high tide will be and were placing bets on it. There is a time zone change here and we had passed into the Atlantic zone, plus daylight savings time, and we weren't sure if the ship's clock was on eastern or Atlantic. Anyway it got a little confusing.

We left at 1530 by kedging off with the danforth and as we floated free we hooked the anchor of another yacht and dragged it .After we untangled the anchors and motored around to where we would dock for the night and pick up passengers, Eben informed us that we were overbooked and Gail and I would have to move into Margaret with some of the other crew. Now we have our cabin, plus the cooks' cabin, to clean and put fresh linen on. Everything got done in time to board the passengers but my bunk is a mess and loaded with all my gear, it's raining, I have dishes and I didn't get to see the museum yet. Maybe next weekend. Now the rain has stopped but it's cold and I'm going to bed!

October 7, Monday

Cold, clear and calm. We are leaving at 0830. Everyone is aboard and checked in and we're ready to go.

Aground! The front three-fourths of the boat is floating but the stern is sitting very hard on the bottom. We tried the engine, sails, kedging - but we are stuck solid and the tide is ebbing quickly. We will sit here most of the day and will leave with the afternoon tide. It will take six hours to get to Annapolis so we'll be getting in late and it should be interesting. This is a very shallow bay with winding channels.

Before we left I made a run to the museum store and got a box of sketches of the Chesapeake Bay light houses. Then the lunch bell rang and after lunch we will be doing some maintenance before we float off.

We got underway at 1600 and motored out to Eastern Bay where we put the sails up and we had a glorious sail to Annapolis. The entrance into the harbor is very interesting and we used the classic stop watch method to identify the light characteristics of the channel buoys. We couldn't locate the "spider" and were way too far off to starboard when I finally spotted it with the binoculars. Eben swung the helm over and we made a bee line for it. After that it was easy and we were in pretty good water. Dutch came out in a water taxi as we were putting the hook down and we changed Captains again. Shirley and Eben off boarded for a hotel as they are leaving in the morning for home.

The night was clear and warm. I'm glad the tide set us on the bottom until 1600 so we had this night sail - otherwise we would have sailed up during the day and been sitting here on a hook all afternoon.

October 8, Tuesday, Annapolis Harbor

Another clear sunny day although it's still pretty cool. We had a chance to hit the showers as all the guests are ashore until 1030 when we will leave for the Solomon Islands. This is a 12-hour run so it will be another after dark landing in a strange area - good practice.

We finally left Annapolis at noon and had a beautiful sail to the Solomons. The entry through a tricky channel was in the dark with unlit day markers. There was reflective tape on the day markers so we lit our way in with flashlights – an interesting maneuver! We finally tied up at the dock at 2300.

October 9, Wednesday

We spent the day in port while the guests explored the town. Ethan stopped by and volunteered his car to run errands for the ship. We found a real powerful flashlight for Dutch - he doesn't want to make another dark landing using the crew's penlights. We visited the *Dove* at St Mary's but just missed Will Gates as he was over visiting the *Harvey*! I got back just in time to do dishes and go to bed.

October 10, Thursday

A dawn start and a beautiful sail into the Choptank River. After winding our way up a very snaky channel we set the hook in 13 feet of water - at high tide - and ferried everyone ashore for a tour of some museum. I ran the tender until 1800.

I found a horseshoe crab shell that looks like a piece of tin. There are beautiful stars tonight and I brought Arcturus down into the trees so it was easy to see against the dark. Lots of people looked at it and got all excited when they located it. We have one hour watches all night. Heavy dew and fog closed in at 0230.

October 11, Friday

Anchors away at 0800 .Greg was running the show in a rather heavy-handed way, giving orders while holding a cup of coffee in one hand and his pipe in the other, so I stayed aft to help wipe the dew off the cap rails for a while until Dutch sent me forward to help out. There is no wind so we are motoring. We dipped our colors to a Coast Guard boat with a big crane on the stern.

We had to motor all the way to St. Michaels and then tie to the dock bow in so we wouldn't go aground again. It started to rain so we put the tarp up and I'm on watch tonight.

Our Captain and first mate have military backgrounds and they are feeding on their fantasies. They give the impression that this is a navy ship and they are treating the crew that have been sailing this boat all summer without them like they are green, newly-enlisted crew that don't know anything and need constant supervision. This is causing all kinds of hard feelings and if the cruise was for any more than two weeks I think half the crew would quit. They even have long conversations about which ribbons they can wear to show their rank. The combination of the two has clicked in such a way that they are starting to run the ship like a military organization. I think they were both pretty low on the totem pole during their service time and now that they have made Captain and First Mate it's gone to their heads and they are playing the power game. The one-up-man-ship is feeding on itself with and it is driving the crew to distraction. It reminds me of the neighborhood kids playing at soldiers or Peter Pan in Never Never Land. It's really kind of funny and pathetic and would make a good play except we have to live with them.

 The last first mate we had was always right in with the crew pulling his weight and more. He took his turn in the chain locker as well as being in the rigging setting sails. Greg just gives orders and likes to tell the crew to do the job as they are doing it! He has been relieved of all the regular ship's chores so doesn't help with dishes, heads or making up bunks. Morale is getting bad.

We off-board tomorrow and then do a ship turnover so we are ready to board again on Sunday.

October 12, Saturday

Cabin turnover. Afterwards Dutch called a big meeting in the saloon for the crew to clear the air and express their feelings. I hope the air is cleared a little but I'm afraid it all went right over Greg's head - he doesn't seem to realize he's the fly in the ointment and Dutch is sticking up for him because he is his first mate. As for what Greg says – that we are just a lazy green crew that won't take directions from him - I hope no one walks. He's not worth it. Today was pretty good and except for some sarcastic remarks from Greg things went pretty well.

The harbor has been filling up all afternoon with both powerboats and sailboats that are coming to spend the weekend. It should be a hot town tonight. I've promised to buy Dan a beer.

October 13, Sunday

Sunny day. I called Eben and when I hung up I was thinking about so many things I left my fanny pack on top of the phone booth. It wasn't even ten minutes when I missed it but it was gone already. There were a lot of boat people waiting in line to get into the showers so I suppose one of the transients took it with them. I checked the lost and found and left my name and the name of the boat but it will be two weeks before we are back here. I sure hope someone turns it in. I liked that day pack and there was around $100.00 in it too.

October 14, Monday

Up at dawn and gone. We had a good sail until 1330 when the wind turned SE and now we are motoring right into it. It's very slow going and we'll probably make a late, dark docking again. We had high haze with sun dogs and high cirrus - we'll see what tomorrow brings.

We finally arrived at the Solomons at 0330. We motored right into a 20-knot wind fighting a flood tide and were making about nine-tenths of a knot until the tide turned and we got up to all of 1.9 knots. We were on a watch schedule with three watches, one hour on and two hours off all night. It was freezing cold when we started out but it gradually warmed up as the wind came up. We are sleeping in Margaret for this trip and it's quite a bit noisier and a lot bumpier than back by the engine in our old cabin. We have quite a bit of up and down motion here. But it really is nice sailing at night and I love being out on the water at night. The stars are spectacular tonight.

This night sailing is good, too, because I'm becoming more familiar with the light configurations. We had a tug pushing ahead on one side of us and a huge tanker on the other, both upbound, but no one got too close. The tug pushing ahead even had all the regulation navigation lights with the flashing yellow on the bow of the barge.

October 15, Tuesday

Up at 0700. It's overcast and there is a report of some bad weather in the offing. We will know better at 0900 when Dutch hears from a friend of his that is checking the forecast. We hung around all day, taking turns at the one shower in town, washing clothes and taking naps to catch up on the lack of sleep from last night. At 1700 we finally left the dock and are now hanging on a hook at the entrance. We will wait here where we have a better exposure to the bay to see what the weather will do. I guess there are two fronts vying for space and we will have either a strong south wind with one front or a strong NE wind with the other one. Meanwhile we wait. The *Ticonderoga*, a big wooden ketch, is anchored just around the corner from us apparently waiting to see what the weather will do also. They passed us last night in the dark.

At 2200 we headed out into the bay and had a west wind for a while. At 0200 Gail and I had watch and just as we got on deck the wind piped up, switched to the north and got cold. Five of us dropped the main and fore and we flew down the bay at 7-8 knots under staysail alone. We came to that little jag off the south shore of the Potomac River and had fun winding our way through a traffic lane around a five foot reef that has a big red sector rotating light house sitting out in the water. To make things even more interesting we had a big ship and a "three white light" tug with a barge flashing its yellow light coming at us on either side. Dutch contacted both of them and we agreed to a one whistle and two whistle passing.

The seas started to build as the night went on and we were really flying. By 0500 when we went off watch we both crashed. At 1100 the winds had built to a steady 25 gusting to 30 and as we turned around Thimble Shoal light we couldn't make head way up the James River under power alone. We raised the fore and had a fabulous ride at 8.5 knots under foresail alone. We sailed past Fort Monroe and up a little creek to downtown Hampton where we tied to a floating dock. This is the second time I've been around Thimble Shoals Lighthouse and both times have been screaming, cold and wet! I hope this clears up for the day sails.

October 17, Thursday

We woke up to pouring rain and strong north winds. Gail and I are back in our cozy cabins next to the engine. It's a lot quieter and I feel at home here. I hope we can stay this time. We got a tour of the town from one of the passengers that lives here and I finally got my driver's license renewed. I have watch today so I'll be hanging around here all day. They have a great old carousel about two blocks from here and it's supposed to be running but so far it's been closed every time I walk over there. Hopefully I'll get to ride it before we leave.

Captain Lane Briggs stopped by with a welcome basket of fruit and he may be able to get me aboard the *Ocean Star* tomorrow after our day sail. It's very cold and windy yet.

October 18, Friday

Sunny and warm. We had 39 passengers aboard for a day sail. All sails set and wallowing. We passed within 100 yards of a lethal looking submarine and he really put out a wake. We also saw lots of Navy ships, including an aircraft carrier with lots of helicopters and other military activity.

We hit a buoy! I'm sure glad I wasn't at the helm or on watch at the time. We got back in at 1600 and tied up. Captain Briggs stopped back to tell me the *Ocean Star* has left so he stayed and watched "Yellow Beard" with us and then invited me out for a drink. Dutch, Greg, Lane and I went out with him. We got back to the boat around midnight and Captain Briggs went back to his boat. We found his hat in the saloon this morning and I will try to get it to him before we leave.

October 19, Saturday

Sunny again. We picked up the laundry after hosing down the decks. Another 40 people boarded for a day cruise and again we had very little wind but it was warm and sunny. Arrived back at the dock at 1600 and a couple of the passengers from the trip down stopped in to say hi and stayed till 1830. Early to bed tonight.

October 20, Sunday

George and I hadn't been to the museum yet so Dutch gave us the day off to go. It was a great day and we got a tour of Fort Monroe and saw the moat and all the fantastic fortifications before we went out to the museum. We got back a little after 1600 and had a quiet evening. If the wind is right we will leave at 2300. Gail and I went for a walk along the waterfront and then called it an evening. No change in the wind so we will stay here tonight.

October 21, Monday

Beautiful pale sunrise with Venus and Jupiter huge in the East. Chilly but not much wind. I got back to the boat after my shower, just in time to make a head count, and we're off.

There were two sailboats anchored in the middle of the river just off our beam and as we did a 180 to head down river we backed onto a mud flat and got stuck! We kedged off by passing a line around a piling on shore and it didn't take much to move us but the engine alarm bell went off from overheating.

We motored out to the HC buoy in the up bound channel and set all sails - we can hold a fair course for a change. The *Spirit* came in from the Atlantic and crossed our bow. Dutch called them to find out how they were making such good time and found out they had their engine on! Some kind of a deadline they have to meet.

We did a cannon salute with a flag dip to a CG buoy tender and then the wind veered around and died. At 1500 we passed the Wolftrap Light and I was relieved of the con until 1800 when Gail and I will have the watch for three hours again. Looks like another all night sail. It should be nice if it doesn't cloud up since the moon is almost full.

I got up at 0230 and it was a great sail. Not much sea but just enough wind to ghost along under a full moon and a brilliant display of stars. Orion was up in the east and with the bright moonlight there was almost a horizon. The lights on shore shone in multi-colors and off to starboard the deep channel flashed its red and green signals. Big tugs with barges flashing their yellow lights are all lit up with triple white, red, and green running lights and the fishing boats are decked in all their special lights plus having their decks flooded with bright white working lights. At 0600, just before the moon set between the rigging and sails we turned the watch over and hit the sack. It was a magical moonlight sail even if it was a little cold.

October 22, Tuesday

We arrived at Solomons around 0800 and as we had just gone off watch we could lie in a nice warm bunk and listen to the docking. It's sunny and warm here and all the passengers have gone off to visit the museum. The *Dove* is supposed to be here today and I'm looking forward to seeing her again along with Josh and Will Gates. She pulled in about dusk and parked up river from us.

October 23, Wednesday

Slept like a baby and woke up at 0600. We loaded the cannon and lay in wait for the *Dove* to come down the channel. We finally spotted her masts moving down through the trees on the other side of an island and when she came alongside we gave her a cannon salute. She didn't answer and when we found she was out of powder Dutch sent some over so she could answer our salute.

After we cleared the red nun buoy off Cove Point we raised sails and are now ghosting along in a light following wind and fog. Dutch lowered the tender and took some passengers out to get pictures of both boats together. We are barely moving and have a long way to go. The sun is shining but not enough to burn off the fog and we have only about a half mile visibility. We are two phantom ships in our own little world ghosting along in a small circle. We won't get to St. Michael's till late again.

The helm is mine coming in and it's a good feeling to con the ship into port past a series of buoys with someone else doing the navigation. Dutch took over for the actual docking and brought her in neatly. Another dark landing at 2230 and I have the watch.

October 24, Thursday

Pea soup fog. I took a hot shower at 0600 and after breakfast checked for my fanny pack - no luck. Goodbye fanny pack and $100.00. I guess I really didn't expect someone to turn it in - it disappeared too fast. We toured the *Bill of Rights*, our sister ship that is tied up next to us. She takes kids that have bad trouble with the law and puts them to work on the boat.

We left St Michael's at 1130 as the Nantucket Clipper is coming to park where we are. We have about a quarter mile visibility and are moving slow with two bow watches, radar and the radio. Reminds me of Maine. We should be in Annapolis around 1630.

After we got out into the bay itself, the fog lifted and we could see about a mile. Two skipjacks were heading up to Annapolis and sailed alongside us for a while. They are headed up for the Chesapeake Appreciation Days celebration that we will be taking part in.

We arrived in Annapolis at 1600 and as we sailed past the Naval Academy we shot the cannon and dipped the flag. We have done more cannon shooting and flag dipping in these two weeks than we did all summer! I haven't heard so many cannon shots, horn signals and radio conversations in one day before. Dutch sure likes to play the signal game. We salute everything with a cannon and signal every change of course - if everyone did this it would sure be noisy. Oh well, it's fun for a while and he will be gone in three days now.

The moon is still full tonight and the red lights on the radio towers are especially bright tonight. We made a run into shore after anchoring but there wasn't any mail yet. The package from Eben should be here tomorrow. Just about everyone has gone to town but it's nice out here on the boat. We watched the Naval Academy give a concert and a performance by their crack rifle drill team as we ate dinner on deck. They must have been practicing for a half time football show.

October 26, Saturday

The fog was thicker and heavier than I've seen before and there are boats all over out here. We took a day cruise out into absolute minimum visibility and can hear their motors and people talking but can't see a thing. Every two minutes our fog horn goes off and like an echo we get answers from all directions. There is one crew member stationed back by the horn button with a stop watch to do the signals. He's lying on his back flat on the deck with the stop watch in one hand and the fog horn button handy to his other hand. Tough duty. Nothing on this ship is automatic.

We motored up the Bay to where all the festivities were supposed to be today. The tide was flooding, and as we got close to the channel going under the bridge we were watching very closely for the opening, but the tide had set us to port so we almost missed the channel. The bow watch spotted it in time to turn away from the pile of cement and rocks at the base of the bridge abutment and we made it through safely. This is really spooky out here. There are twin bridges here but the fog is so thick we can't see both of them at once. When we passed under the first span I could look up and see the bottom of the bridge but nothing else, then nothing until the next bridge started to materialize out of the mist. These bridges aren't very far apart but the mist is thick.

At 1500, just off buoy # 2 outside Annapolis harbor entrance, in pea soup fog, a 41-foot CG patrol boat pulled up alongside and asked permission to come aboard. Bill Shamel, the chief warrant officer, and the CO of the Annapolis Search and Rescue station, stepped on board and asked for me! Captain Dutch called me up to the deck from the saloon. He had just sent me down there to get something so I assume this was all prearranged as a surprise. The CG 41-footer eased up to our side and Chief Shamel stepped aboard. He wished me a Happy Birthday and presented me with a beautiful bouquet of flowers shaped like a sailboat with an American flag flying at the top of the mast and a ship's bell buried in the bottom of the basket. How's that for class! Rob must have pulled some strings to accomplish that. It's not often anyone gets a bouquet of flowers delivered by a 41-foot CG patrol boat in the middle of a fog bank!

I would love to be up in a helicopter watching all these boats milling around in the fog. Most of them don't have radar and there are some that don't have a compass or radio aboard. A whole parade of boats formed up behind us to follow us in, like a mother duck with ducklings, but there were all kinds of calls asking the CG to tell them where they were. It really was kind of funny out there with all those boats ghosting around blowing their horns and yelling. One thing good is that no one goes fast enough to do any damage even if they would collide.

Ethan and Beth brought me a cake and wanted me to go out for dinner but as I had watch tonight I told them I couldn't go. The cooks had baked me a cake too and everyone sang happy birthday.

Molly from the Bay of Fundy trip stopped by this morning to return some of the photos from that trip and stayed on board for the day sail. She gave me a fantastic picture of the bubble feeding and a bottle of rum. A very nice birthday.

October 27, Sunday

Fog again! Eben's sister and friends slept on board last night. At 1000 we have all the passengers aboard for the cruise today and Dutch had given his introduction and safety speech .When they tried to start the engine it turned over a couple of times and then just clicked! The lister was on so they let the batteries charge for a few minutes and tried again. It almost started but the power ran down very quick and it started to click again. Dutch, Buddy, Dave and Greg played with all sorts of different combinations that didn't get any results. No luck. The batteries are dead!

The lunch was served on deck and after they were done we took everyone back to shore. The cruise is over and we never left the anchorage. I did have a nice talk with Linda and Frank Schmeer as she will be on the celestial navigation trip to Bermuda.

 The dynamic duo are still playing with the motor, changing wires around and making sparks. Sure glad this is diesel and not gas! Eben will be aboard tonight and he isn't too happy about a few things.

October 28, Monday

At 0545 a loud thump woke me up so I went on deck to check it out. It was still dark and a cold front was passing through with a very brisk north wind. The wind was pushing the boat down hard against the anchor, and that is what woke me up - the boat hitting the end of the rode as it pulled it tight. All the fog has blown out over the bay where it is still hovering like a huge dark cloud. The moon and Venus are brilliant in the dawn sky. I went back to my bunk and listened to the anchor chain stretch and strain against the wind.

Eben got up and had the engine running in about 20 minutes.

This morning was spent being the tender driver and running people around to do their errands. At 1300 we boarded about 50 of Eben's friends and went for a great sail on the bay. The fog has lifted and the north wind is giving us a great ride.

There was a soft thud as we went aground on the mud just by the spider buoy. Eben had given the helm to one of his friends and wasn't paying attention figuring he knew where he was but we weren't driving very hard so Eben backed it off without any difficulty.

We tacked back and forth below the Bay Bridge and then headed back to Annapolis to set the hook by 1700. Dinner was served on deck and everyone seems to have had a good time. It's only 1900 but I feel like it's midnight.

October 29, Tuesday

Clear and cold. I have the job of cleaning and adjusting 11 sextants that will be used for the class. This took all day and most of them seem to be in pretty good shape. Three still need some gluing and there are some parts coming from town but we will have one per student.

There is a Hurricane off Bermuda. We are listening to the SSB at 0600 and 1800 for the Atlantic weather forecasts. There are 55-70 knot winds and 35-50 foot seas. I'm glad we are sitting here at anchor. The tides are so high that the docks are almost covered with water and the parking lot at Fawcet's is starting to flood. Tomorrow we will start plotting the west wall of the Gulf Stream on the big plotting sheet that we will use for our DR track on the passage.

October 30, Wednesday

Clear and cold again. It's a beautiful sunny fall day and I went into C. Plath *(a retailer of ship supplies)* to find some parts for the sextants and the dividers. The dividers were fairly simple to fix after I soaked them in oil to get them apart. Now with the new parts we have seven good sets of dividers for the class. I walked from the Charthouse all the way over to the capitol building and finally found a Jew's harp for $1.75 that has just the right piece of metal to fix the last sextant. Looked at a model of the Blue Nose Schooner at the same store Kim bought me the model of the Skipjack for my birthday last year. It's a fascinating store with model trains and lead soldiers, model boats and all the fun stuff to build them. He wants $ 95.00 for the model I want so I guess I'll skip that.

I took the water taxi back to the boat and fixed the one sextant with the Jew's harp piece and glued the other two. Tomorrow I'll mail a lot of excess baggage up to Rob that I don't want to carry back on the plane. I also have to mail Captain Brigg's hat back to him as we missed him in Hampton.

We plotted the storm on a hurricane plotting sheet and tomorrow we will plot the Gulf Stream for sure - we missed it today. Every morning now at 0600 the SSB comes on and we tape the weather and then play and replay it until it's all copied down. It's almost a different language and takes a while to tune my ear into the sounds. Once we have the coordinates for the storms we plot them. I really like doing this stuff.

October 31, Thursday

Spent the whole day doing piddly jobs. The tide is so high from the storms that the whole bay looks like it's ready to overflow - like a glass of water that is filled right up to the brim and if you lay a finger on the rim it will spill over. There are all kinds of storms out in the Atlantic north of here and up by the Cape into Boston.

I'm running the tender and just took a boat load in for showers. At 2000 I'll go pick them up. I'm tired tonight and getting another cold sore - just what I need now that we're getting ready to go off shore. We leave in three days and the deck is covered with all kinds of projects. One half of the deck has been tarred with some sticky black gunk and tomorrow we move everything over and do the other side.

I'm making a couple of birch plywood navigation tables to store in the head and use for the class to plot on. They have to be sanded and varnished. It's clear and cold tonight and the stars are sure bright.

November 1, Friday

More chores today. Put a coat of varnish on the navigation tables - they are just flat pieces of plywood but it takes a long time to put a smooth coat on them. Made a run into C. Plath to pick up some mirrors for the sextants but they don't carry parts for sextants - they send them out for repair.

We have three new gals as crew and one new guy. Rich came back at noon and it's sure nice having him here. Dutch stopped out to show Rich the log book with all the loran coordinates for the buoys on the way down the Chesapeake. He has been taking readings off our loran as we sailed down so they will be very accurate.

I've been trying to chart the Gulf Stream on some universal charts but keep getting interrupted. It was cloudy this morning but it's cleared up and is very calm. The tidal surge at the mouth of the bay is 10 feet and here in Annapolis the docks and the streets along the bay are under-water. They must be used to this here though because they have metal signs that read "Caution - High Tide."

November 2, Saturday

The wind changed in the middle of the night to the south so it's pretty warm here this morning. They dropped me off at a laundromat to do the ship's laundry and finally after four hours came back to help me carry it back to the ship.

We have had three guests aboard so it was a mad dash to get the cabins cleaned and the passage crew settled in their bunks. Missed both lunch and dinner but I'm really not hungry. We got most of the cabins ready and settled out the books to send with Eben. I'm $36.00 over but Eben says not to worry, that someone will claim it.

Called home and they have had 23 inches of snow in the last 24 hours!

We leave tomorrow night for Bermuda. The weather sounds pretty good with a stationary high keeping things stable for now.

I finally got the Gulf Stream plotted and was working on the cold front when it got hectic again. Right now we have 14 crew, three early navigation students, and a couple of guests milling around. The cooks are in the saloon stowing food in every available nook and cranny. There are crew working on rigging, woodwork, deck engines, and bilges. The whole ship is full of activity. Eben has freight for people that are already down in the islands, and that has to be stowed in the forecastle and lazaret - the whole boat is stuffed!

The foot for the fore topmast is being replaced so there has been crew working way up in the rigging.

Lots of traffic in here this weekend. Annapolis is a busy harbor and I think a lot of them are "snowbirds" heading south for the winter. The racing school is finishing up their season and the whole fleet of J boats parades by twice a day as they finish off their final regatta. They look like a flock of butterflies out on the bay in the afternoon sunlight.

Open Ocean

November 3, Sunday

I finally got into town to get some supplies for the trip. We have all the students aboard and we're all fueled up and ready to go. Buddy wanted to sign on with us in the worst way but the crew list is filled out so he will have to stay here. Dutch has decided to fly down ahead of us to line up a winter job before that season gets underway.

At 2100 we are on our way; it's a good thing we're heading south as the water is not the place to be when it gets this cold - it's very penetrating. It's supposed to get down to 20 degrees tonight. There's huge seas reported off the Atlantic coast in Maine but the storm system seems to be all north of us so I hope we are in the right window to make the shot out without hitting any storms.

I'm now the assistant celestial navigation instructor and as such, have been relieved of crew duties. It seems strange not to be part of the crew anymore and be able to stay below and work on navigation instead of handling lines and being on watch. It's kind of nice but I miss being in on the boat handling.

November 4, Monday

I slept like a baby last night; only once in the middle of the night I heard Gail come in off her watch but went right back to sleep thinking it was nice not to have to stand watch.

The boat developed a slight rocking motion some time early this morning so I figured the wind had picked up. At first light I stuck my head out and it looked nasty! The wind is strong out of the north with whitecaps on cold gray water and it is cold. We just passed the traffic lane off Smiths Point so we're making good time. We are under staysail alone now but they are getting the foresail ready - we will round up to raise it and then fall off. If it draws okay on this course we'll cut the engine and save on fuel.

Breakfast is still at the second sitting but as soon as that is cleaned up we will set up for our first class. Dave will give the first lecture this morning and run through how to read the nautical almanac. He really gets into this teaching. The tape recorders aren't working but I copied the coordinates of the west wall of the Gulf Stream as the computer read them on the SSB.

As I sit here on my bunk I can hear the water gurgling right on the other side of the hull next to my ear. The ship feels alive as she sways and rocks on a downwind run with a five-knot following sea. The shaft break is nonfunctional and there is a high pitched whine as the propeller and shaft keep spinning even if it they aren't in gear. The clothes hanging over my bunk alternate between laying flat against the hull or swinging out over the aisle. We are making excellent time but the seas are really building and it's a question now whether Rich will push out into the North Atlantic or duck into Norfolk harbor for the night.

At 1500 we passed through and over the Chesapeake Bay bridge and tunnel and are in the Atlantic Ocean - right in the middle of the lecture on increments.

November 5, Tuesday

Not quite as cold today but still overcast and blowing. The seas are magnificent with big gray swells topped with masses of clean white whitecaps. The greater shearwaters are swooping and circling around the boat and it's great to be out here again.

We are in the Gulf Stream! The water has changed to that deep cobalt blue and it turns ice blue under the breaking white caps. We took the water temperature and it is 75 degrees. The boat is still creaking and squeaking, rocking and rising. A complete place setting just flew off the table and slid across the saloon sole, and it is of vital importance to hang on to glasses of liquid or they land in someone's lap. We are really moving - up to 9.1 knots for a while and holding around eight knots.

As I was standing at the rail watching the spectacular swells, the wind would blow warm as it came off the water and then turn cold again. I love it out here and doubt that I'll be able to stay away from the ocean for any length of time.

At 1630 I stuck my head up through the hatch after class and there was the sun right off the starboard quarter, big and red, setting in the clouds: Beautiful. It's starting to get warmer but we are still rocking and clanking. There is a tear developing in the foresail so the storm staysail was hoisted on the main and the fore was taken down for repair. We are now running the engine to charge the batteries.

At 1930 we seem to be through the Gulf Stream and the seas have settled down a little. The mainsail is raised and that has helped steady the boat. The stars have arrived but there are so many of them and there are still big globs of clouds floating around them that I'm having a hard time identifying anything but Cassiopeia. The wake caused by our passage is full of flashes of light again and it's starting to feel warm. It should be beautiful tomorrow.

November 6 Wednesday

At 0300 I woke up and we are still rocking but it's a much gentler roll. After making a notation in my log of the loran coordinates I poked my head topside and it's warm! There are still dark puffs of clouds but Venus is up bright in the east and Orion is complete in the south. There is a faint light from a ship on the horizon to the north of us but otherwise the ocean is empty. The sea is black without any white caps. We have slowed down as the wind dropped off and the ride is a lot easier.

It must have been very frightening for people coming from Europe to head west through this warm area of the ocean and then run into the rough passage at the west wall of the gulf stream only to have the air and water turn frigid. No wonder they thought they were coming to the edge of the world.

We started the day with star shots at 0500. The horizon was hazy to the north but I got a clean LOP with Venus. When the sun came up we started shooting sun sights and reducing them. Fourteen students on deck shooting the sun and then trying to do sight reductions and plotting on the saloon tables is interesting.

At noon it started to haze over and by 1600 it was raining. We are being pushed south of our DR track and the loran signals are getting pretty weak. The water is still warm and that very deep cobalt blue, very clean and clear where it breaks for our wake. One small flying fish is all I've seen so far; but not being on bow watch all the time cuts down on the sea life I spot.

About 2330 a squall came through and there is a gradual building of seas so we are starting to rock and roll again. The pitch of the engine increased a little and the sheet for the foresail slid across the track over my head with a couple of loud bangs as a wind change came through. Some things flew off the shelf in the galley and as I went out to pick them up and stop the noise from the rolling around, Rich came down the ladder and beat me to it. His foul weather gear is wet and shiny so it's probably raining.

The course read out on the loran is 220 so we have either turned and are running ahead of the storm or we are being blown that far off course. We should be steering around 120. We are back to pitching again but because of the engine noise I can't hear anything else except once in a while there is a thump as a wave slaps the hull and the beams squeak and creak as the ship rolls.

November 7, Thursday

Rich headed up to drop the foresail and raise the storm trysail and now, running under staysail and trysail, the motion of the boat has settled down to a smoother roll but I still have to brace myself so as not to fly out of my bunk. I'm very happy to be down here this time rather than up on deck -

although when I'm up there I find it very exhilarating!

At around 0400 the wind veered around to the SW enough so that we could tack over and start heading back in the right direction. At 0800 I was on deck enjoying the ride on the bow when I was informed that it was to become the men's shower room, so I left. Shortly after that a squall came through with 25-knot gusts and pouring rain. I got my hair soaked and it felt good.

It's a majestic sight watching a squall approach. Dark solid clouds with a change in the color of the water to a deeper blue as the wind kicks up small waves in front of it. The sea fades into the clouds as the rain gets closer until everything is a solid mass of driving rain and the horizon disappears in a blur of rain and wind. The squall passed over quickly and didn't get a chance to build any seas - just a rash of whitecaps for a while. The skies are still overcast but it's getting lighter.

Right before lunch the sun came out and everyone came on deck: either taking sunshots, using buckets of salt water for showers, sunbathing or just generally enjoying the first warm sunny day we've had. Pat and Dave gave us a song fest with a guitar and mandolin. At 1500 we had another class and I'd hoped we could get some good star shots tonight, but no stars and so to bed early.

November 8, Friday

The wind picked up in the middle of the night so I built a blanket dike to keep me from rolling off my bunk. I got a very hazy sunshot before breakfast and a little clearer one a little later. Dave is down with the flu so I had the morning class and I finally got a running fix with two sun lines. We've had sun and rain showers all morning and the seas are fairly heavy.

DOLPHINS! Lots of them diving all around and swimming with the boat. They are brown with mottled sides and they don't look like Flipper at all. They must not be the bottle nose, but they aren't the white-sided dolphin that we saw off Maine either. There were big and little ones and they would swim alongside the boat and then dive under us to come up on the other side and behind us.

I spent the rest of the day working up shots for a test. This is a good way to give the students practice; I just hope we don't change speed or course in the next 18 hours or my APs will be off.

November 9, Saturday

No stars this morning as the majority of the sky was overcast but there was a break in the east and the sunrise was spectacular. The sea is a mass of small hills and valleys with no real rhythm to the waves. The larger swells that fling the bow up and down are throwing green water over the caprails. With the overcast sky and the sun slanting through the clouds I feel like I'm in a molten bowl of pewter. I finished plotting the problems for the test before breakfast and then used my Hylex bleach bottle and 100-foot line to check our speed: six knots.

The students started plotting the problems and it seems I "took" the shots way after dark. They thought that was funny! That's what I get for working the shots backwards. At least we know they are learning something if they spotted the mistake. When there are no stars you have to do something.

I've put the time for spotting Gibbs light on Bermuda at 2130 GMT. We have a betting pool going. Someone claims to have seen a sea turtle but of course I was below and didn't see it, though I did see some more flying fish and dolphins today. The dolphins played in our wake and didn't get close enough to really see but they looked bigger and blacker than the ones we saw yesterday - almost like a minke whale.

Gibbs light showed up at 2100 - I was a half hour late on my time. We must have picked up speed? Anyway we are now under sail and cruising on a starboard tack about 25 miles north of Bermuda. It is beautiful! All the stars are out, the swell has flattened out, and a warm breeze is blowing off the land, just enough to keep us moving. It's great sailing out here and looking up at the red over green lights way up in the rigging with the stars weaving back and forth as we rock in the gentle swells. I still can't believe I am actually out here in the mid-Atlantic after a seven-day passage on this great schooner and about to sail into Bermuda! We will sail out here for the night and go into St. Georges in the morning. It's a very narrow entrance with lots of coral reefs and wrecks around. About 2300 we hove to and it took a while for me to get used to the new motion. Quiet as we lay off the wind, and then violent up and down as the sails push the boat into the wind, until we stall out again.

The Caribbean

November 10, Sunday

We got some star shots at dawn and the sunrise was magnificent. As we tacked into St. Georges through the narrow cut in the rocks, a man swam out to meet us and yelled and waved at Rich. They made plans to meet later.

About half way through the cut the wind was blanked by the land and all the sails went slack. We glided on through with the ship's momentum until we cleared the high banks and the sails filled again. Out in the open harbor Rich headed up and the sails were dropped and "harbor furled."
We were tied up by noon at the customs dock. After we went through customs some of us walked out to Tobacco Beach on the other side of the bay. We kept picking up more of the crew as we walked along and ended up at a bar that is built in an old fort.

I left everyone at the bar and started back to the boat but ran into Dave and ended up at another bar where I was propositioned by a Portuguese from the Azores. I finally left (alone) and came back to the ship.

I like Bermuda so far: the temperature isn't too hot and the water is beautiful and there are some fantastic volcanic rock formations on the north side of the island. As the lava hit the water it must have bubbled as it cooled because there are large pits and holes in the black rock that form weird and wild shapes.

November 11, Monday

The wind woke me up. The rigging is whistling, the hull is squeaking against the big heavy tire fenders on the pier and waves are slapping against the hull. It's a beautiful day on deck with the sun just coming up and a warm wind blowing out of the south. All the buildings on the island are pastel or white and everything looks clean and fresh. Lots of banty chickens and goats on this island; I can hear the caws, clucks and baas most of the day. Last night the dark was filled with a chirp from a little frog that lives in the trees and its voice is much bigger than he is. There are people sleeping all over the deck but that can be uncomfortable as there are sudden showers at any time, day or night.

Instead of taking the bus for a tour I agreed to go by moped with Dan, Josh, Greg H., and George B. The five of us rented mopeds and had a ball! They took off like banshees and let grandma trail behind but they stopped and waited for me every once in a while. About 18 or 20 miles down the south shore drive we stopped and went swimming in the surf at Elbow Beach. Beautiful clean water and pink and white sand. When we got back to the boat we hit the bars with about 15 of us crew and guests.

November 12, Tuesday

It's a beautiful calm sunny day - the front has passed over and a lot of the boats that have been waiting for this window will leave today. Two of our students, Norm and Pat, have decided to leave the Harvey and crew for a couple on a smaller boat; they feel they have learned celestial sufficiently and want to experience a 41-footer which is closer to what they will be sailing themselves. There are a lot of boats looking for crew. One man I talked to that was looking because his crew jumped ship here in Bermuda; another guy came this far singlehanded and decided he wants help for the rest of his trip. Bermuda seems to be a real cross road for sailors and ships. A Swedish boat came in late last night with a broken mast, and another from Nova Scotia with a broken boom. We did have some pretty good winds.

Tomorrow we load the last of the new students and hopefully leave for St. Thomas. It's HOT!

November 13, Wednesday

I went for a walk around town this morning and mailed Eben the ships' bookwork for the week. Checked the cabins over and got everyone signed in and settled down. We ran through a series of drills for fire, man overboard and abandon ship. Everyone is all checked through customs and we're waiting for the duty free booze to be delivered to the ship.

We got underway at 2100. The weather has cleared, the wind is out of the west, and the moon is half full. I fell asleep before we had cleared the channel.

November 14, Thursday

We are having a very bouncy ride because we have to ride in the trough. The wind is right out of the west and pushing us in the right direction but as it's a beam reach we are rocking and rolling again. We're making excellent time, the sun is out and it's a great day though if it doesn't get any warmer it will be fine with me. Class starts at 0930. Dave has his fishing pole out again with a big silver spoon on it. I hope he doesn't catch any more sea gulls. It took three of us and lots of the gulls' blood to get the last one unhooked.

The Celestial class is underway again. Delano, one of the students, fell last night sometime and cut his eye. When I saw it this morning he had a bandage over it and it looked bruised and bloodshot. Around noon he announced that he was seeing floating spots.

We have turned around and are heading back to Bermuda. We were 18 hours out so it'll be at least 18 hours back. We're losing two days and every one is a little put out and worried about flights.

November 15, Friday

We arrived back in Bermuda around 0830 and Rich asked me if I would go to the hospital with Delano. We took a taxi into Hamilton and spent the morning at the Emergency Room and in doctors' offices. They are very good here, efficient and thorough. The emergency ward doctor wore

Bermuda shorts and a tie! It turns out that Delano has torn his retina so he is going back to the states to have it operated on. It's a good thing we brought him back.

It's another beautiful day and the wind was just right so Rich had us raise the sails in the harbor and we sailed through the cut out into the ocean and are heading south again. Course 180 for 842 miles! As we got halfway through the cut we lost the wind in the sails but there was enough momentum to carry us through again

Everyone seems to be in a better mood now that we are underway again and we had a good class this afternoon. We covered plotting and how to use the sextant. We had a good wind for a while but now the engine is on again and we are pushing south, trying to make up for lost time.

November 17, Sunday

Another beautiful day and I got a great 3-point fix with Betelgeuse, Venus and Sirius. The morning twilight was beautiful with millions of stars and the planets were huge. We have been motoring in dead calm with huge swells that are probably left over from that big storm up north.
At 1000 the breeze freshened so the sails are up but the motor is still on. It would be nice to cut the engine but we are still trying to make up the lost time.

The students are getting good and I think they have an excellent grasp on sight reductions. Now it will be hands-on practice and one-on-one tutoring. I'd like to go swimming and Rich says the next calm we'll have a swim call. We'll have to rig up the fire hose for showers again pretty soon. It's cool and balmy tonight, there is a light wind out of the NW and we are moving along nicely. We'd covered 254 miles as of 1800 today.

November 18, Monday

The wind has picked up and we are flying along in front of some spectacular running seas. The boat is rolling and rocking as we slide down the front of huge swells: maybe only eight to ten feet but glorious! The sun is shining out from behind big white puffs of clouds and the sea is a deep cobalt blue with breaking whitecaps all around.

We have a tiny little bird on board; I hope he stays with us for a while as we are at least 400 miles from anywhere. Saw some flying fish today with deep, deep blue backs. A beautiful glorious day. The class went well again today and Dave is using most of my shots. The moon was so bright tonight we could have gotten shots way after sunset. It's about three-quarters full and lights up everything. There is a psychology discussion going on in the saloon.

November 19, Tuesday

Star shots again this morning and I got a good fix. Although I'm still a couple of miles different from Dave we can at least see each other from our fixes. My plotting sheets are getting pretty impressive as I'm taping them together to make a long scroll of 870 miles. It's another great day with sun, wind, and a downhill sleigh ride. We are rocking and rolling again with the wind out of the NE. I can't believe this weather and I'm going to hate to leave this ship, but I don't like the sound of the winter schedule and the heat.

November 20, Wednesday

No stars to speak of this morning. I peeked out the hatch just before dawn and everything was overcast so I went back to bed. We are still screaming along and have averaged eight knots for the last eight hours: that's 68 miles from 2200 last night to 0600 this morning. The shaft has been turning all this time and it sounds like a motor that is always running so this morning Rich wrapped (very carefully) a heavy rope around it about 6 times and when it was just right he pulled it tight and the shaft locked up. Ah, the silence! No more vibrations or noise. We are still rocking and sliding downhill and back up over swells. I can't believe how perfect this sail is. The water, sky, wind: everything is perfect and tonight we have an almost full moon that's already up. But my shots tonight are a puzzle: they come into a small cocked hat but I'm almost 10 miles south of everyone else including the DR plot.

It's a beautiful night but I think the natives are getting restless: A full moon and days at sea make them ready to party. We're still moving very fast, about eight knots. There was some sudden noise on deck because of a barracuda that Dave caught, but they threw it back before anyone down here had a chance to see it.

I've been doing celestial since before breakfast this morning and I think I'm getting a little burned out. I'm predicting we will see land at 0300 tomorrow - at least the very tip of the mountain on Tortolla should be visible.

November 21, Thursday

Up at dawn to take shots. I got three stars and Saturn, put the sextant away and went to the bow to look for land. At 0645 there it was: big on the horizon, right where it was supposed to be, so I think maybe my shots were okay after all. We will be at Rudy's in Virgin Gorda by noon today and will stay there tonight. I'm ready for a swim and I'm not having much luck concentrating on anything but the islands. We had some dolphins swim with us for a while and a flying fish landed on the deck. Dave caught a beautiful blue marlin and threw it back. We passed Sand Cay about 1300 in a torrential rain that made all the islands disappear, but by the time we were south of Jost Van Dyke the sun was out again and we docked at Rudy's dock in Great Bay. Everyone filed through customs and then I walked the beach to pick shells. After dinner I wandered down to Rudy's and Foxy's and did a lot of dancing with both crew and passengers. Greg H. passed out so Josh and Matt brought him back to the boat. John passed out sitting up at Rudy's. Dave and Greg G. took John back to the boat in Rudy's truck as he couldn't even stand up. I went back to Foxy's after helping to load him on the truck to find the rest of the crew and I'm glad I did because everything went crazy on the boat. There must have been a tremendous brawl as there are lots of repercussions this morning. Rich is apologizing to the passengers now and is trying to explain the situation. Dave, John B., and Greg G. are in deep water.

Nov. 22 Friday

Today we go to Cruise Bay. Our three extra Captains have been asked to leave the ship and sort out their differences. They will come over later on the ferry I suppose.

We sailed over to Cruise Bay and checked through American customs. The ship is anchored around the point from the harbor and we are doing tender runs. In here we can go swimming and it feels great to dive in and shampoo again. I took the last tender run into customs, checked through, and then wandered around town. Rich has Dave's passport and he asked me to meet the 4:30 ferry from Jost and give it to him. When the ferry came in, bearing all three captains, I gave Dave his passport and the message from Rich that he wanted to talk to them. I went back to the boat and Rich had me drive him back to shore in the tender where I sat at the dock waiting while they had their talk. John B. is the only one coming back on board and I can't understand that! I would have let them all go back to St. Thomas on the ferry. Greg is done. He won't be working on the boat anymore and the crew is very relieved. I don't know about Dave. All he said was he had talked to Eben but I haven't had time to learn any more.

November 23, Saturday

We had another glorious sail from Cruise bay back to St. Thomas. A beam reach with about 20-knot winds. We sailed right into the harbor and if the wind hadn't done something goofy at the last minute it would have been a great landing. As it was we overshot and got a little too close to the head rig of the boat ahead of us. These ships don't reverse very well! Nothing serious, just a little excitement for a while.

Dan and I took a taxi to Megan Beach, walked for a while, went for a swim, and then sat in the shade of some sea grape bushes and had a *cold* Pina Colada. I took a cold fresh water shower at the beach and came back to the boat. It's nice tonight as there is a cool breeze but it was sure hot today.

I have my ticket back to the states and will be leaving Monday morning at 9:30.

Torrential rains last night and this morning. Damp and clammy. One of the guests described it as just like having a wet black lab sleeping in his bunk with him. As much as I like this ship and crew, I couldn't handle the weather much longer.

Nov.24. Sunday

Cool this morning (relatively). Most of the guests leave today.

Gail took me across the street where she bought me a drink and then when we got back to the boat there was a going-away party for me, set up with Malibu rum, a great dinner, and a decorated cake. I'm a little overwhelmed. The whole crew pitched in to buy me a 24-karat gold bracelet of dolphins and a very sentimental card.

Nov. 25, Monday

Got up at 0600 and finished packing. The whole crew was there for breakfast and I'm going to miss this way of life. All the crew, the ocean, and the ship. Everyone gave me a big hug and Rich asked me to be here for the passage back in the spring. Dan came to the airport and helped me push four big bags through customs. Now I'm in the airport waiting for my flight to be called. It's very rewarding and a little overwhelming to experience the friendship this crew demonstrated towards me as I leave. I knew we all got along well but I hadn't realized how much they all liked me.

A very nice feeling.

Glossary

Abaft: Toward a vessel's stern

Abeam: At right angles to a vessels fore and aft line

Ahull: Archaic term for the position of a ship in which all her sails are furled and the helm is lashed a-lee, as in heavy weather, so she lies nearly broadside to wind and sea

A-lee: Towards the side of a vessel sheltered from the wind (the leeward side)

AP: Assumed position

Backed: Said of a ship when the wind is acting on the forward side of her sails thus driving a ship backwards

Beam: The width of a ship

Beam reach: A course sailed with the wind coming from almost across the beam (the side) of the boat

Bear/bears: To sail or proceed toward a course or object

Beating: Sailing close to the wind; close hauled

Block: Pulley or a set of pulleys

Boom: Spar used to secure the foot of a sail. It swings back and forth when the ship tacks

Bow sprit: Large boom or spar projecting forward and slanting upward from the sailing vessel's bow to meet stress on the fore top mast stay

Braces: Lines to control a yard

Broach: When running with a high quartering sea, you turn toward it and get broadside by accident, exposing your vessel to the danger of capsizing or shipping heavy water

Broad reach: To sail with the wind forward of the beam but not close hauled

Bulkhead: One of several upright partitions separating various compartments in a water-tight hull. For preventing passage of oil, water or fire from one section of a ship to another

Burton, anchor burton: A line which controls the anchor

Cat head: A long beam that extends out from the ship just aft of the bow

Celestial shots: Using a sextant to "'shoot" a star and bring its reflection to the horizon for getting a "fix" in celestial navigation

Chafing gear: Mats, baggy-wrinkle, battens, etc., fastened on rigging or spars to prevent injury from chafing

Chainplate: A metal plate used to fasten a shroud or stay to the hull of a sailboat

Chop: Short, rough seas, caused by meeting currents or a breeze blowing against a current

Close hauled: Sailing close to the wind; also called "beating"

Close reach: Sailing with the wind coming from close to the bow

Companionway: A raised and windowed hatchway in the ship's deck, with a ladder leading below; also the hooded entrance-hatch to the main cabins

Con: To direct a vessel from a position of command

Course (as indicated by a number, like 100): The point of the compass to which a vessel's path is directed. The direction a ship is steered

Cross bearing: A two position line fix. Two almost simultaneous bearings are taken of two objects and laid out on the chart to give a position

Danforth: A type of anchor using a stock at the crown to which two large flat triangular flukes are attached

Davit: A crane, often working in pairs and usually made of steel, used to lower things over the side of a ship, including launching a lifeboat over the side of a ship

Day mark: A stationary navigation marker in shallow water, usually in a harbor, to mark channels. A large geometric shape atop a pile of "dolphins" (see definition below) to mark one side of a channel or an obstruction

Dead reckoning (DR): Keeping track of a ship's position by recording its time, speed and direction and any external factors that may affect its course. It is the basic navigational information available to the navigator

Depth sounder: An electronic device that measures the depth of water under the boat

Dingy: Small boat

Dividers: An instrument used to measure a distance between two points on a chart, similar to a drawing compass

Dolphins: Logs or wooden pilings driven into the seabed in shallow harbors or bays for extending above the water to mark channels

Down wind: Sailing with the wind over the stern.

Draft: Depth a vessel sinks when afloat, as measured from waterline to bottom of keel. Depth of water required to float a vessel.

Drydock: Any dock in which a vessel can be hauled entirely out of the water for repairs or painting

Fall off: Dropping leeward of the required course

Fenders: Any material suspended against a ship's side to prevent damage or chafing

Fetch: The distance the winds or seas can travel without obstruction

Fix: Taking bearings on coastal landmarks or celestial observations. Where the bearings intersect is called a fix. Or, the ship's observed position

Furling: To roll or gather a sail and secure it with gaskets to its yard or boom

Gaff-rigged: A boat rigged with a four-sided fore-and-aft sail with its upper edge supported by a spar or gaff which extends aft from the mast

Gaff sail: A type of sail used on a gaff-rigged vessel

Galley: Boat's kitchen

Gibe/jibe: To shift position with a fore and aft sail from one side to the other when the wind is over the stern, a sometimes dangerous but necessary maneuver to change direction

Gunwales: (Pronounced "gunnels") The upper edges of the hull

Halyard: A rope by which a sail is hoisted

Hank, hanked on: A sliding ring that secures the sail's luff to the mast

Hawser: A heavy rope or chain to moor large vessels

Head: Ship's bathroom

Heading: The vessel's course; as in heading NW

Heel: The lean caused by the wind's force on the sails of a sailing vessel

Hook: Familiar term for an anchor

Hove to: To stop a vessel's headway by bringing the wind under shortened sail as nearly close-hauled as possible a little a forward of the beam

"In irons": When a sailing vessel has lost its forward momentum when tacking (changing direction by heading into the wind) making it impossible to steer

Jack line: A single line leading to the boom for keeping the sail, when lowered, from falling on the deck

Jenny: A type of spinnaker sail

Jib: A triangular sail rigged between the foremast and bow

Kedge, kedge off: A technique for moving or turning a ship by using a relatively light anchor known as a kedge. The kedge anchor may be dropped while the vessel is in motion to create a pivot and thus make it perform a sharp turn. The kedge anchor may also be carried away from the ship in a smaller boat, dropped, and then weighed, pulling the ship forward

Ketch: A two-masted yacht with the after (mizzen) mast stepped in front of the steering position

Knot(s): The speed of one nautical mile per hour

Laker: A huge ship that carries coal and other goods on the Great Lakes.

LAN: Local Apparent Noon

Lazaret: A small stowage locker at the aft end of a boat

Lazy jacks: A network of cordage rigged to a point on the mast and to a series of points on either side of the boom that cradles and guides the sail onto the boom when the sail is lowered

Lee shore: The coast lying in the direction the wind is blowing.

Loran: Long range Aid to Navigation. A radio system for determining a ship's position at sea.

Luff: The forward edge of a sail

Main shackle: The shackle at the head of the main sail

Marlin: Roll of twine used for multiple or miscellaneous purposes on board or at a dock

Marlinspike: A tool used in ropework for tasks such as untying rope for splicing, untying knots, or forming a makeshift handle

Marlin twine: A lightweight cord (line) used in marlinspike work

"Off the wind": No longer under pressure of the wind. ("Falling off" is turning away from the wind)

Parceling: Stitching a covering of tar, marline, and canvas to protect the steel mast shrouds from the corrosion of salt water, often as high as six feet off the deck

Pan-pan: Urgent radio message relating to the safety of a ship or person

Piling: Timbers driven into the seabed near a dock to protect the boat and pier from colliding. Usually these are wrapped to protect the hull, and have some give to them

Plot, Plotted: Marking a ship's course, speed, and direction on a chart.

Point of sail: The direction a vessel is moving. When the wind is dead astern it's called running with the wind or sailing free.

Reaching: Sailing a tac with the wind from between the stern and the beam. (See also broad reach, beam reach, and close reach.)

Point high: Pointing too much into the wind so that the sails luff and you lose speed

Port: Left

Pulpit: An extension, usually a heavy plank, beyond the bow of a boat.

R.A.C.O.N. buoy: Radar reflective buoy used to aid navigation

Ranges; range markers: Pairs of lighted or unlighted fixed aids, when observed in line, show the centerline of a channel

Range lights: Lighted ranges

Red Nun: A type of navigational buoy, often cone shaped, which marks the starboard side of a channel.

Reef (in a sail): To shorten sail by reducing the area exposed by rolling the sail or tying in reef points.

Rode: Anchor line. It may be fiber, chain, wire, or a combination. Usually the bigger the boat the more chain is laid out.

Running: Sailing with the wind. Often considered a poor choice of tac

Running block: Adjustable hardware for control of spars and sails

Running fix: Two bearings are taken of one object with a reasonable time between them. The distance traveled and the course of the first bearing are transferred giving the position of the vessel at the second bearing

Sampson posts: Two posts that rise vertically from the deck of the ship at the bow, used mostly for anchoring.

Schooner: Fore and aft rigged vessel with two to six masts, with the foremast shorter than the main mast

Serving mallet: A wooden device shaped like a mallet, grooved on the bottom, and used in serving ropes and pounding tar into chinks

Sextant: Navigational instrument used to measure a ship's latitude

Sheet: A rope used to control the setting of a sail in relation to the direction of the wind

Sheet in: To pull on the sheet adjusting the position of the sails

Shoal: Shallow water

Shrouds: Ropes or cables serving to hold a mast upright

Single side band radio: A type of 2-way radio using amplitude modulation

Spar: A wooden pole or, in later years, also iron or steel, used to support various pieces of rigging and sails

Spinnaker: A large sail flown in front of the vessel while heading downwind (also called running with the wind)

Sprit rig: A less common but often very useful alternate sail rigging

Spring line: Standard dock line used to control the fore and aft motion of a boat made fast to dock or float.

SSB: Single side band radio

Starboard: right

Standing rigging: The fixed shrouds and lines which hold the rest in place

Stay: A strong line or cable supporting a mast, and leading from the head of one mast down to some other mast or other part of the vessel; when running from mast to hull to the fore it is a forestay, and when aft a backstay

Stay rigging: Wire or line used to support the masts in a fore and aft direction and to carry certain sails

Staysail: a triangular sail set inside another headsail making a sloop into a cutter

Sunline running fix: Using two celestial sun lines, taken at least 45 minutes apart and advanced along the ship's course to fix the ship's position

Tack: The forward bottom corner of a sail. To tack is to bring the wind on the other side of the sail when beating up against the wind

Block and tackle: A system of two or more pulleys with a line or cable threaded between them, usually used to lift or pull heavy loads

Tender: A vessel used to provide transportation service for people and supplies to and from shore for a larger vessel; sometimes called a ship's tender

Throat: In nautical usage, a funnel or narrow passage

Turnbuckle: A device for adjusting tension in stays, shrouds, and similar lines

Up wind: Going to windward; going towards the wind

V berth: The bunk at the bow of the boat

VHF Radio: Very High frequency. A very high frequency electronic communications and direction finding system

Walker Log: A device used to measure the speed of a vessel. The most popular type is manufactured by Walker

Warp: To move a vessel by hauling on a line or cable that is fastened to an anchor or pier or tugboat

"White hull": A small rowboat, sometimes with a sail, employed as an alternate means of transportation from boat to shore

Windlass: A winch mechanism, usually with a horizontal axis and crank. Used where mechanical advantage greqter than that obtainable by block and tackle is needed, such as raising the anchor on small ships

Windward: In the direction from which the wind is coming

"Wing on wing": Running with the wind behind so that one sail can be set to the right, the other to the left

"Worm and parcel with the lay, turn and serve the other way": A ditty to remember how to protect a section of line from chafing by first laying yarns (worming) to fill in the voids between the wrapping line, then wrapping marline or other small stuff (serving) around it, and stitching a covering of canvas (parceling) over all

Worming: Laying yarns between the line voids (see immediately above)

Yard: The horizontal spar from which a square sail is suspended, or a dock or shipyard

Yardarm: The very end of a yard, as in to hang "from the yardarm," and the sun being "over the yardarm"

Yawl boat: A small rowboat suspended from davits at the stern of the boat

Made in the USA
Middletown, DE
04 October 2023